NEW PLAINS REVIEW

Spring 2015

Editors and Staff

ᕷ

Executive Editor	Shay Rahm
Production Chief	Michelle Lee Waggoner
Editors-in-Chief	Maggie McGee
	Brendon Yuill
Managing Editor	Kavon Kahkesh
Poetry Editor	Hyunjung (Crystal) Kang
Assistant Poetry Editor	Kaycee Chance
Fiction Editor	Lindsey Chadwell
Assistant Fiction Editors	Jessie Layfield
	Mary Inselman
Non-fiction Editor	Anna Hester
Assistant Non-fiction Editors	Adalee Shuck
	Andrea Hall
Webmaster	William Andrews

ᕷ

New Plains Review Publishing Group
University of Central Oklahoma
Edmond, Oklahoma

NEW PLAINS REVIEW

ISBN-10: 0983735778
ISBN-13: 978-0-9837357-7-9

New Plains Review is a literary journal published each academic semester, sponsored by the English Department, College of Liberal Arts, at the University of Central Oklahoma. The image found on every cover of *New Plains Review* issue since 2000 is based on a painting titled "Phantom Warriors" by acclaimed Native American artist and UCO alumnus Sherman Chaddlesone.

New Plains Review
English Department, Box 184
University of Central Oklahoma
100 North University Drive
Edmond, Oklahoma 73034
(405) 974-5613

newplainsreview@gmail.com
www.libarts.uco.edu/english/newplains

Submission Information: *New Plains Review* accepts original work in prose, poetry, drama, fiction, art, and photography. Submissions are accepted by email. For editorial guidelines, please visit the website.

Ordering Information: Pricing for subscriptions, current and back issues are available through the website.

IMAGE CREDITS

Cover Art
Counseling a Daydream (Front)
Central Park (Back)
Nicholas Perry

Section Feature Art
Annie Doan

Special Section Feature Art
Central Clock in Winter
Michelle Lee Waggoner

Foreword

"That is part of the beauty of all literature. You discover that your longings are universal longings, that you're not lonely and isolated from anyone. You belong."

— F. Scott Fitzgerald

The *New Plains Review* staff, a student-run literary journal at the University of Central Oklahoma, is proud to have received hundreds of submissions from all over the world. Keeping with the University of Central Oklahoma's goals of both excellence and diversity, it is our mission to share with our readers a selection of fantastic works from a diverse number of authors and artists throughout the world. We are eager to help these creators broaden their audience and re-inforce the importance of the arts in our everyday lives. It is also with these hopes of transformation and a broader perspective we present the Spring issue for 2015 to our readers. These selections give a glimpse into the authors and artists minds be they depictions of coping with everyday life, either in the past or the present, or growing more aware of the world at large. The works selected in this issue of the *New Plains Review* and its special "UCO@125" section strive to show glimpses of the human experience from a variety of different times and viewpoints and the ever evolving human spirit.

This year, the University of Central Oklahoma is celebrating the 125th anniversary of its opening. As a result, we have added a special section to this issue of the *New Plains Review,* which is dedicated to the celebration of "UCO@125." The University of Central Oklahoma is one of the first institutions of higher learning to be established in Oklahoma; as a result, it is one of the longest running universities in the southwestern United States. The University is still going strong today, and it is dedicated to instructing through the methods of transformative learning. This method aims to not simply teaching students, but to teach them through opening their minds to other possibilities and viewpoints — to not only make them better scholars, but to make them better people.
We hope that our journal is an inspiration to all our readers.

Sincerely,
Maggie McGee and Brendon Yuill
Editors-in-Chief

Contents

FICTION

SPECIAL SECTION: UCO@125

NON-FICTION

ABOUT THE CONTRIBUTORS

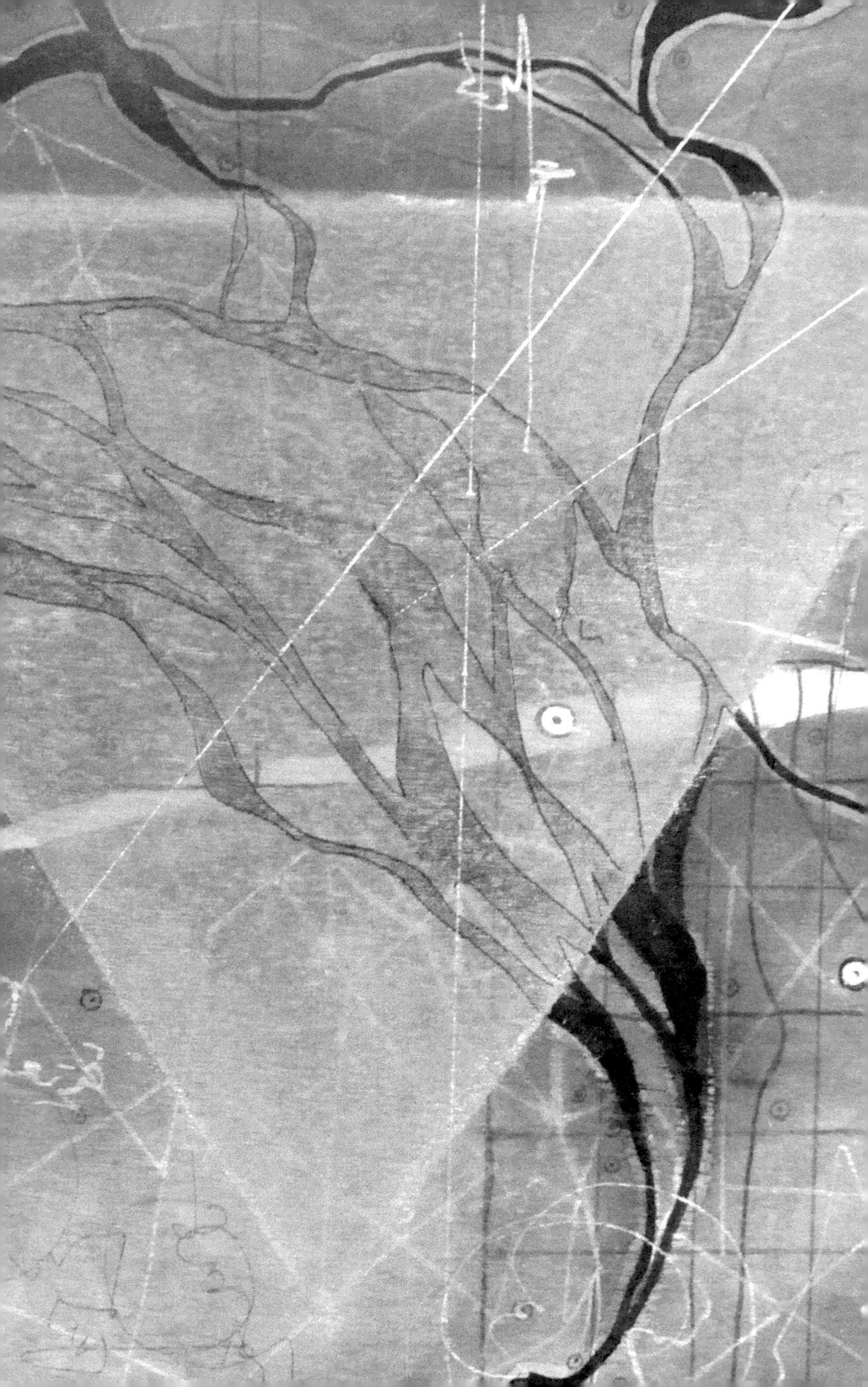

POETRY

Grace

Erren Geraud Kelly

Who moved through the café

Like an apparition

Who lingers in my head like

Grace notes even when

I don't see her for months

She is a graceful cat

Thumbing through the papers

And sipping her coffee

Gracefully, the sun comes through

The café windows

And cast a light on her breasts

I look at her and I'm graceless for a moment

As if I wanted to say more

A graceful cat

Plays a C note

As she walks off the piano

And into my dreams

*

Simon Perchik

You come by though the hole
has no other place to go
waits behind this ice-packed dirt

left over from when the sun

had no choice either, spreading out
as emptiness, the last resort

— this hole must sense it will die
the way the sun died, was buried
in the open, alone, circling down

strangely quiet with nothing to cling to
except the endless under and under
just to reach winter, to lift

and care for it — you visit the left out
built from years and years
but you are asking the impossible

with just your fingers — on tiptoe
would make it easier, anything
would make it easier.

A DAY OUT

Benedict Downing

Dripper swallows the gushing water,
electrocution contacts to silver the liquid,
molten bubbles pick up the plant's granulated beans,
one, two drops start a puddle,
a notebook collects
coffee stains, records on my notes,
hand in hand with forgotten drafts.

Two red cushions,
four pearl pillow cases, used to be called white,
whitening, chlorine water and powder detergent,
papers lie about the quilt, neatly stacked in order of appearance,
pen superseded by the keys and moving cartridges,
the briefcase needs to be filled and carried away as we part the pad.

My dirty laundry set to appear on the machine,
colors of the days past, assembled in a swedish plastic basket,
chinese made, light and everlasting,
sweat spreads to the bottom, a need
to punch hours of pains.

The air conditioner spurts out the cold,
three of us, behind desks, in front of computers,
silence broken by the puerile yawn of the secretary,
an utterance follows, a cruel schoolyard gag joke,
the bully, flips slides, pictures of his mistress,
to call up high school 'dude' days.

The bus ride, sudden stops, thrust and hold,
the window is large, five or ten absorbed or rinsed out,
people busy, on watch a small screen, goldcoins
generated in Farmville, cross action on chats,
tuned or saved TV drama soaps,
if only glance upward to rise from their seat for the elders,
the flip-book is everlasting.

The neighbors in front chant their daily rants,
extended family on two floors,
crying five year old gives to a rooftop cat's lament,
alley ends to the stay-at-home four hundred pound son,
wrapped in towel, water dispenser full, charging stations
on, my hand grazes the chest beating the silver coated shaking,
an upright hand that likes to stretch out, a grabbing
of cloudy notions, passage through the mountains,
dirt gravel and cement, jars line up in front recyclable waste,
plastic bottles and metal canisters a humped lady picks up,
a younger couple arrives on scooter,
a wax frog as guardian for the open terrace,
clothes hang from the roof, shoes stack on the perimeter wall,
in the empty fish tank, they stored outside, lives a plastic bag
filled with paraphernalia gill survival.

Mind's musing tour contaminates the rustling motors on the main road,
past the zebra crossing, to grow a beard, that will
be shaved next morning, a reading sums on a clear glass table,
my feet to stare at, a motorcycle that spurts out of the alley,
the clothes line to fill in front of the window.

Avocados and Avocadon'ts

Laryssa Wirstiuk

You worry one day he won't look at you
the same. You'll lose the ability to swathe
commands those eyes burn into your skin,
to dress them with fine knee-high socks;
open, cashmere cardigans; black tights —
oh, what magic a lavish bandage can do.

Preening for others, you'd never possessed
such precision, never delivered a response
to a request obvious as a flame: "Wear this."
You had guessed at their wants: cleavage,
ass. But he's more specific than that.
You've never liked being told what to do.

Except by him. This is not a submission
or a forfeiture of a feminist card: you are
a pupil of someone who has paid more
attention than you, now paying attention
to you. You want to be called "beautiful"
forever, yet doubt it's something he can do.

He likes other things about you, of course,
and compliments a timeless trait: your ability
to choose fruit. From experience you know
all about "avocados and avocadon'ts."
He doesn't see you in the grocery store
testing ovoids the way a urologist might do.

At home, you cut open for him the ripest one
while he puts hands on your hips and holds you
together. Maybe this slicing is one thing
you can teach, but he just wants to appreciate
the way you move with a knife in your hand.
You've seen pictures: what knife to face can do.

But what good is this talent when you can't
fondle yourself then meet his lips with your best
as he asks, "How do you do it?"? You just do.

Catægis

Addison Eaton

Never fall in love with a hurricane boy.
He's got chaos in his veins,
And skin that tastes like sea salt
Hemmed with destruction.
The eye of his storm
Will clash with the love you harbor.
And the idea of his tempests
Grazing your beaches
Isn't nearly as beautiful as it sounds.
Gale force lips travel
Down your storm ravaged spine.
They will be your end, your maritime destiny.
Yet by then you will have learned
There's a reason hurricanes are born with human names.

Tempestas

Addison Eaton

Fall in love with a hurricane girl.
For she's a blue-eyed tempest, with sun kissed hair.
She's chaos and passion
And kisses like an angry, unbridled storm.
The energy she holds within,
Could rattle even the strongest of sea monsters.
So lay aside all qualms
That her slender frame isn't strong enough
To handle the monsters inside of you.
Learn to love this beautiful water nymph within the storm.
Pull out your maps and study the currents of her hips.
Discover why sailors have fallen for her siren song since adolescence.
Perhaps then you will learn why
There's a reason hurricanes are born with human names.

Forgotten

Priya Prithviraj

There's a scented silence here,
that's broken only by the ticking of the kitchen clock,
and the sound of rain.

As I sit by the window,
watching drops of rain chase each other
down the windowpane,

a cup of warm tea sits on the table,
forgotten.

Buzzing Beneath the Leaves

Clayton Adam Clark

– *Centennial Park, Nashville, Tennessee*

Music gambols off a stage
between two trees greater around
than any bass drum or the country-

gospel-jazz-blues that unloads
from bruised amps. *We're lucky to have
this weather,* the emcee reminds us

between sets. The park is something left,
not made, its oak trees thriving like rests
before strummed chords. A tree I don't recognize

flutters with heart-shaped leaves not shaped
like actual hearts, but the lean of its trunk
reminds me of my backbone's compression.

The man our emcee identifies only as Rico
dances all songs at the stage's foot.
His fingers explode for crash cymbals,

his back pumps from hunch to upright,
clavicle-wrenching chorus, and his dreads
are plaited like a scarf or a thin blanket

that covers his spine when he stills
between songs. The frequencies must survive
inside there, trapped and shaking the bones

that rivet him at rest. After a while, mothers
allow their children to dance with Rico. He needs
the band, the band needs a crowd, the crowd

wants nothing but to dance, and he teaches.
One boy dances facing us: back-flips,
high kicks, robot, the worm. He's good,

but his moves aren't driven by the drums.
He grooves alone in the mass like the two giant
oaks, their roots seizing the earth to hold plumb.

They'll savor the rain, just not today.
The music doesn't fill this boy
as it does the pit-shaped crowd, all buzzing

beneath the leaves at the same pitch,
but someday if he's lucky he'll feel it
and the earth's reining us in, rain

the prodding reminder that we share
one course of movement. A fountain
in the man-made pond keeps algae lapping

at a stone wall instead of overcrowding
the water. The ripples preserve the surface:
I can see some sky and trees reflected.

Infestation

Ty Stumpf

I stand books across the shelved headboard of our bed.
The Holy Bible, which I only thumbed through,
War and Peace, which I read every word of,
Moby Dick, which I will never read,
Shakespeare's Complete Works, which I half-read,
and eighteen others lean right
like stopped dominoes.

They die daily.
The dust chalking
their outlines on the shelf.

On my nightstand, the wood is slick.
Tiny prints scurry across
and nest in the middle.
These piled books are lived in, few sole or whole.
Fractures and folds spread across their covers.
The pages flutter with rips, pictures smeared,
corners worn round, nibbled soft.

Our daughter climbs into our bed, laughing
at her book before we've even opened it.
She leans against my chest. I close my eyes,
begin the first sentence, and she takes over
singing the story like a song.
Her brother charges into the room,
diving onto the sheets in his improvised wolf suit,
bouncing on the bed until I call him "wild thing" and promise
he can choose next.

As our children wrestle,
their books scamper across the floor,
under the dresser, in the closet,
like mice caught by a flipped light switch,
alive, quivering, and ready to brave the open room again.

Memorable Envy

Carol A. Oberg

I see from here
In our company
filled home
The snow fall
light and thick
Straight down
a magical cleanser
Shaking down
from the sky so later
When I do sneak out
the clean cold air
Will burrow into my coat
hold onto my skin so
I will carry its freshness
back inside
For everyone there
to stop what they
Are doing and
for a pensive moment
Wish they were me

Low Blood Pressure

Lauren Marshall

I'm surrounded by high pressure
people, who balk at my touch
or my trembling, or my scars
from standing under hot
water that I cannot feel
until it's burned.

My morning runs
are a distraction
from teeth clicking
like a keyboard and
the apathetic kettle
that teases my patience.
Endorphins numb cold,
and I can sit and read
a book for at least an hour
before my feet and head
notice microscopic waves
of cool in the air.

I can only bask in the afterglow
of sex for so long before the
covers need to be pulled
over my salmon body
and my lips, plump oxytocin cherry
must bury themselves in
a steadily pulsating Adam's apple.

My nose is a dog's nose,
and it drips at any temperature
less than twenty degrees.
I like dogs, small ones,
the ones that shiver in the rain
despite their coat of hair.
I let them in the house
and we cuddle,
dreaming of dancing puddles
and the cleansing qualities
of Mother Nature's tears.

I'm Frankenstein to Mom and Dad,
who have to watch their sodium
intake and alter their meat and potato diet.
They're stingy on heat in Winnipeg winters.
They make up for it
by purchasing me a new house coat
every Christmas.

I made the mistake of researching
my blood pressure,
the deadly biology behind
the skin my Grandma called porcelain.

I'm a romantic, and I love
in that way, but sometimes
I can only be grateful that *someone*
is there to watch my shallow sleep,
lest my tepid heart fail.

tracks

Jonathan Cooper

we stood under neon lights
                sagging, sour
in a long hallway bracketed by hospital beds
                unused, poised for the onrush.
Out of a sunken, swaying face he talked parallel tracks,
                a thousand thousand
in his vast depot of worst cases,
                what ifs, what ifs,
and told me he was anxious,
                craving crystal meth —

"though, you know, what you say makes sense to me
                as I listen to it."

But as his eyes flicked, I saw his mind move
                beyond, beyond
my small offerings about serenity,
                staying in the moment;
like a passenger on a high-speed train
                who nods, who nods
at the beauty of a copse of trees
                as he rips past
on the intransigent rails of
                perfect, perfect reality.

SEPULCHERED SHIP

Lana Bella

Above the rolling darkened sea, a solemn silhouetted ship floats
Tracing the wide-reaching horizon such a heather lingering ghost
And startlingly the echoing tolls stirring the stilled mooring boats,

Checkered moon drapes the surfaced pane a pale reflecting gloss
Where its faint shadow coils the rotting mass of sepulcher's fros
And darkly prowls the unlit deck a stony man pregnant with loss,

One tiered sail casts down upon the spiring mast fanning the sky
Darting seagulls nestle near where the aged stern dips and glides
And the wind shakes loose the curdled haze by the starboard sides,

Then the stoic sea clouds over and down the pouring shards of rain
Streaming its droplets cold gushing wide the raw achromatic mane
And coursing his upturned face wetting through the blue smoke's vein,

Where comfortless dusk seeks refuge in the whipping silvered storm
Just as the fretful man brushes clear the rolling beads in swift alarm
And the single sail bends in floppy wake shorn of its queenly charm,

When a bitter front sweeps the idling ship towards the remote shore
To the grainy jagged earth by the ebbing harbor tranquilly moored
And his speckled face spews of unfurled ache a chilled torrent roars,

The arced yellowed moon tears in flakes laying bare its innards' woes
Brittle alabaster sand chases through the hourglass in chamber gold
And winged vanished doves reflect in his eyes at the far chasm's hole,

He aches for a muffled sleep of empty breaths between wakeful bells
So by the sloping bow the auspice sea loops a noose of mortal hell
And anguish hooks its fatal claws in the grave stitched of garland veil.

Departure of the Summer Heat

Richa Gupta

I hear the crunch of shriveled leaves
disintegrating beneath my feet
I watch the remnants blow with the breeze
as I plod to the morning, jungle heat

I grimace at the crow's menacing calls
as its blown off course by a summer squall
My legs entangle in the irksome vines,
a massive web, clumsily intertwined

The streams reflect a dismal, leaden brown
a surging, rushing cascade as its source,
the dreary shades mirror that of the ground —
the soil-rich, yielding, or sand-dry and course

Trickles of sweat pour down my face
my heart pounds wildly at an aching pace
My ears prick nervously at the most innocent noise,
I whirl instinctively, my body poised

The warm shades of exotic vegetation and creatures
offer no consolation to my itching eyes —
miniature blue-eyed insects with inconceivable features,
with a striking, tropical, imposing guise

I feel the lapping ripples of a gleaming pond,
as vivid schools of fish tickle my knee;
they thrive underneath the abandoned fronds
of ferns, and the lime green creepers stemming from the tree

And as the softer tones of the strident sun
are veiled as the latter sets over the horizon,
unobtrusive critters return to their knolls
while joy and freedom has been triggered in my soul

Some say people feel vulnerable at night,
as they are unfortunately denied the sense of sight
Yet, it simultaneously means the withdrawal of heat
a one-that-cannot-be-compared, stimulating treat

I hear the crunch of fresh, crisp leaves
harmonizing beneath my feet
I gape as the remnants swirls patterns with the breeze
as I gallivant to the night time, frosty heat

I welcome the birds' mellifluous calls
as they swerve motifs by the sudden squalls
My legs are offered warmth by the obliging vines,
a convoluted web, flawlessly intertwined

The twinkling streams reflect a golden brown,
a buoyant, effervescent fall as its source,
the vibrant hues indicate that of the ground —
the secure domain of animals — safe and sound

I appreciate the shadowy views, the sublime scenes
of the foliage, that have turned ebony from green
Though humans are declined the perception of sight,
in summer, the most wonderful experiences are lived at night

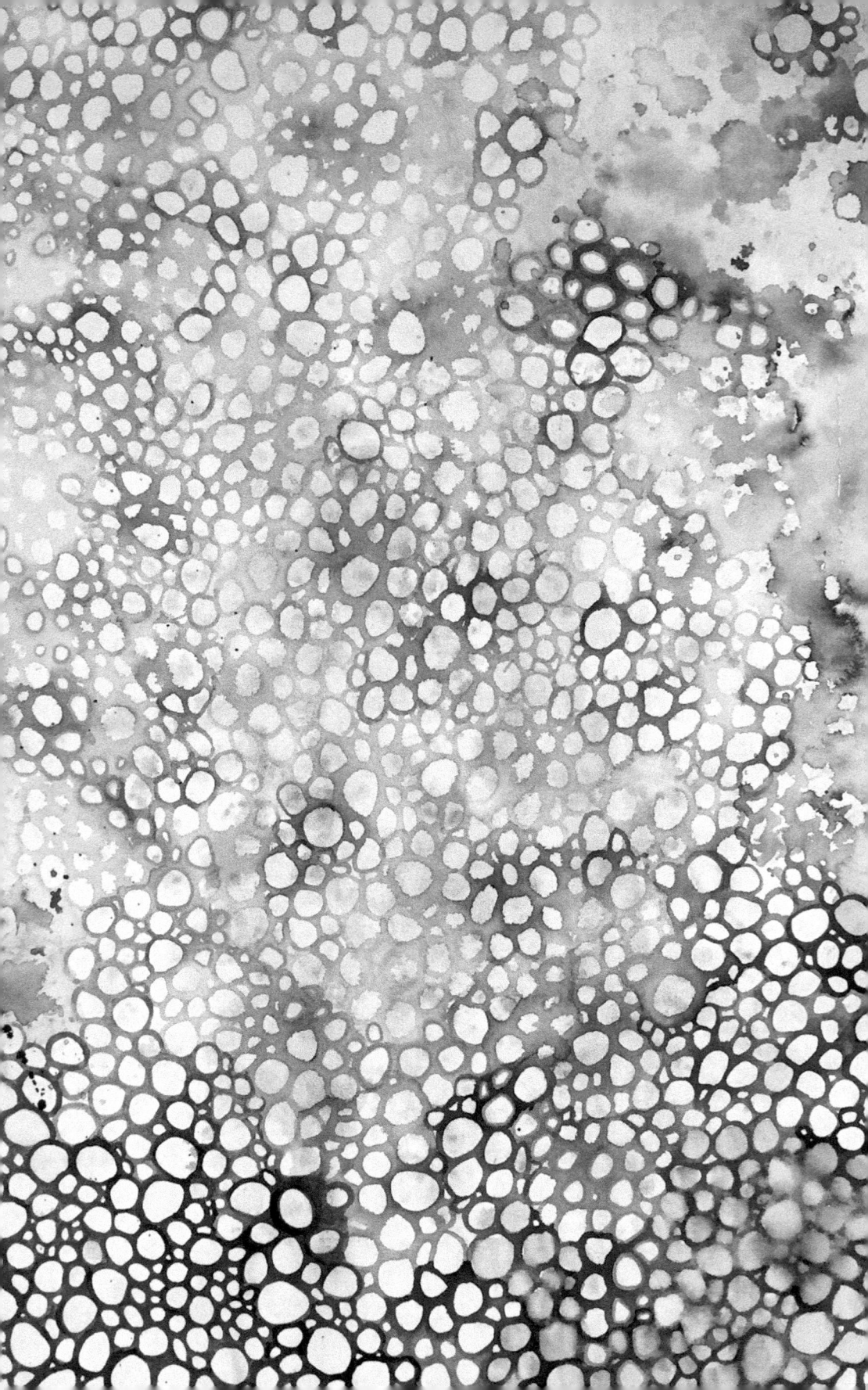

VISUAL ART

Berlin, Germany, Holocaust Memorial

Sarah Katharina Kayß

London, United Kingdom, Underground

Sarah Katharina Kayß

City Life
Woman Holding Cat

Allen Forrest

Ink on paper

City Life
Men Sleeping on Bench

Allen Forrest

Ink on Paper

FICTION

Hadamar Ashes

Tammye Huf

A spider crawled up my sleeve, but I didn't move. Instead, I stood at attention as the officer fixed the pin to my jacket. Pride bubbled up in my chest and threatened to leak out of my face, but I'd learned self-discipline, so I pushed my smile down into my chest, where it glowed red. My mother and sister watched from below the platform in the second row after the party leaders, and I imagined their pleased faces and straight backs. My father over in Poland and my uncle in France would find out soon, when the letters reached them, and they would boast about me. Me. I could feel the corners of my mouth threatening to pull up. I breathed out slowly and smoothed my face, conquering my emotions.

As the pin sat gleaming on my chest, the officer talked about how important the Hitler Youth were, what an excellent role model I would be for everyone in the program, and how impressive it was that I'd been made area leader at seventeen. I stood ramrod still for the whole thing, my eyes never leaving the flag. Then we raised our right arms and lifted our voices for Fatherland and Führer.

My first big task was to reappropriate the Jewish properties. The Liebermans and the Rosens had moved out at the beginning of the year, in the middle of the night like thieves. Everyone was glad they had gone, except Old Man Dickopf. He wouldn't shut up about how Lieberman's father saved his life in the Great War, and how they were as German as anybody else. I told him that Dieter Großlöch's dog saved *his* life, but it's still just a dog. I told him what our teacher said about them not being the same as us, and how the teacher had called Josef Rosen up to the front of the class to show us all the differences. You couldn't tell unless you really looked, but when he showed us like that, it was obvious. Old Man Dickopf said I was as blind as "that Hitler" that I worship. He actually said, "that Hitler." After that, I decided he didn't need me to help him understand, he needed someone to teach him some respect.

We decided to turn one house into our Hitler Youth headquarters. The village hall had been good enough before. But as the war got bigger and bigger, and the officers counted on us more, we needed a place of our own where we didn't have to clear out for the next group coming in.

The other house we dedicated to the war effort. We would use it to store donated supplies and to house soldiers passing through. I put the League of German Girls in charge of keeping it up to scruff.

The last property to deal with was the Jewish cemetery on the hill. A few of the boys thought we could just build a house on top of it, but who would want to live on top of dead Jews? In the end, we decided to pen it off and let Jürgen Schneider use it for his sheep. Some people thought that was wrong, but most agreed that the Schneiders deserved a break. Their son, Andreas, had been in our year, he'd even been our friend, but then he got kicked in the head by a horse. At first, they thought he wasn't going to live, but he did. Except he wasn't normal after that anymore. He talked gibberish most of the time now and acted strangely, but at least he could walk and talk. He couldn't join the Hitler Youth, of course, and with his mother gone, his father couldn't join the army, so nobody in that family could contribute to the Reich. That's why people thought they shouldn't get the land, except it's different with Andreas. Before it all happened, he was one of us.

⊷

In the fall after I became the area Hitler Youth leader, my sister Klara started at a new school in Boppart. She rented a room with a local family, and I barely saw her anymore. Whenever I could get away, I rode up to see her on my moped.

On my fourth visit, I met her friend Ursula. She was beautiful and full of life, and I left three hours later than I had meant to on that first day. Then, I started visiting my sister more frequently. Then, I started visiting Ursula.

I thought about her at school, at home, at the Hitler Youth head-quarters, everywhere. I would be writing my report and stop halfway through, wondering what she was doing, what she was wearing. My mother laughed at me. She said I was acting like a schoolgirl. Maybe I was.

When Jürgen Schneider came to see me, I'd just had a letter from her, which is why I wasn't really listening when he said it the first time.

"A search party," he repeated. "To find my son."

"You know he likes to wander off," I said. "He'll probably be back in a few hours."

Herr Schneider shook his head. "He stayed out all night. Andreas would never do that. Something's happened."

I folded up the letter. Andreas panicked in the night if he wasn't at home by dark, which meant he was lost or trapped or hurt, and defi-nitely frightened.

"Yes," I said. "A search party. I'll get everyone together."

We spent the afternoon combing our village, the next village over, and the land between. We found nothing and had to call it off once the sun set. Old Man Dickopf turned up and made everything worse, tell-ing people Andreas had been turned in and taken away. Herr Schneider shouted at him to shut up. I'd never seen him so furious.

I sidled up to Herr Schneider and spoke softly, like I was taming a horse. "Don't listen to him. He's always stirring up trouble."

"Why wouldn't they take him?" Old Man Dickopf spat. "Is he a credit to his race? Will he help usher in the glorious new Reich? He was an undesirable and now he's gone."

Herr Schneider hit Old Man Dickopf in the mouth, which knocked him clean over.

"Don't listen," I said. "They would have brought him back. Or told you if they'd taken him to a hospital."

"You've heard the rumours," the man said from the ground. "Do you believe them now?"

"You mean the enemy propaganda?" I spat. "The lies they feed us so that we'll be at each other's throats, just like this? No. I don't believe them. I never will. Heil Hitler, and long live the Party."

I turned him in that night. When they took him I stood right in front where he could see me, so he would know.

In the spring, Ursula told me her mother wanted to meet me. They lived in Hadamar in a large old four-story on a tree-lined road. I left early, leaving extra time for anything that could go wrong, but I got there over an hour too soon. I walked around her neighbourhood, taking off my jacket and feeling the heat of the sun massage my back. She had said there was a nice walk we could take, which was probably the path I found running along the canal. The cool sound of running water rose up to meet the eager heat of the sun with me in between, not knowing which I liked better at that moment.

Eventually I circled back. When I turned onto her street, the air grew heavy. It tasted spoiled. Through the canopy of leaves, a few pale flakes dropped to the street, and as I drew closer to her house, the flakes fell like snow flurries, but without a winter crispness in the air, and the flakes not quite white. I thought they might be coming from the trees, but the street was lined with ordinary oaks.

Ursula opened the door as soon as I walked onto her first step. A smile split her face, and she was just beaming at me, looking like an angel. I wanted to kiss her so badly at that moment, I didn't dare move.

"You look beautiful," I said.

She blushed and skipped down to me at the bottom step to take my hand. That's when she saw the flakes and gasped.

"Oh, no. I didn't know they were doing it today. I'm so sorry. We never know when it will happen." She tugged me hurriedly toward the door.

"Doing what? What is all this?"

"Ashes."

I looked at her, expecting her to explain, but she hustled me inside and closed the door.

"Mother made cheesecake," she said. "We can eat before we take our walk. It should be over in an hour or so."

Her mother appeared at the door, shorter than Ursula but much more imposing. "It's very nice to meet you, Franz, but I just need Ursula for a minute. We have to take the wash in quickly before everything is ruined by the ashes."

"But where do they come from?"

Her mother glanced at Ursula and then back at me. "The psychiatric hospital is just up the road. Come, Ursula."

They hurried out back with me standing there wondering what that had to do with anything. Then, a wave of understanding crashed over me. The nausea was instant, and I flung myself into their bathroom and over their toilet. I heaved out my breakfast and my lunch, and then I retched out the nothing that was left in me. I wiped my mouth with the back of my hand and pulled myself up. I looked in the mirror and saw that I had gray streaks across my mouth. I heaved a big empty nothing into the sink.

Frantically, I scrubbed at the ashes on my face and hands. They were gone with only a little water, but I scoured with soap, washing three times, splashing water on the walls and floor. I rinsed my mouth out, trying to clear it of the rancid taste of sick. When I stepped back into the hall, I was trembling, deep in my core, off kilter, like the feeling I used to get from caffeine before I got used to it. To my right, I could hear Ursula and her mother in the kitchen, and straight ahead was the front door, and behind the door, the ashes. I took a step toward the door.

"Franz?" Ursula called from the kitchen.

The shaking was bad, so I put my hands in my pockets and sucked in deep breaths.

She came into the hall and took my arm. "Are you ready for a coffee? You'll love my mother's cake. It was my grandmother's recipe."

I opened my mouth to tell her that I couldn't stay, but a noose tightened around my throat, and I stood gaping at her, bug-eyed and fish-mouthed. She led me to the dining room, where her mother served cake and poured coffee. My mouth still tasted of vomit, and when the cake touched my tongue, I almost gagged, but I had learned self-discipline, so I pushed it down and chewed and swallowed.

My Mother's Lipstick

Toby Tucker Hecht

When my mother died, my father continued to live in the upstate New York house they'd shared for thirty-five years, refusing to clear out any of her belongings — even when I volunteered to help him with the chore.

"I want to feel she's still around me," he'd said. "She was so light-hearted about everything, even her illness. A perfect example of how one should live, but how most people can't. I dread the heaviness now."

Five years later, he died suddenly of a stroke, and the task of sorting through the relics of their long married life fell to me, as an only child. I worked for several weeks, giving away or throwing out almost every-thing. Each object had a story, but now those stories would live on only in my memory. There were over fifty pairs of shoes — some decades old, three sets of mismatched dinnerware, and a stack of table linens. I kept a pair of open-toed navy suede pumps from the 1980s, knowing I would never wear them, a dozen embroidered napkins, and a few dog-eared cookbooks.

In a drawer of the bedroom night table lay a lipstick, hardly used, and of a shade of deep pink that had an iridescent sheen to it. It was called Rose Serenity. My mother had been ailing for several years — bed-ridden — and had not worn makeup in all that time, so I guessed the lipstick was at least eight years old. It wasn't a color I particularly liked, but my mother's name had been Rose and although I didn't believe in lucky charms, I slipped it into my shoulder bag where it nestled among out-of-date coupons and business cards from people with whom I had no interest in reconnecting.

When all was cleared out and clean, I walked into each room, caressed the walls with the palms of my hands, listened one last time to the answering machine message in my father's baritone voice, discon-nected the phone and put the house up for sale. The price I was asking was reasonable, and a young family bought it within days. I handed over the keys to the real estate agent, took the bank check from her hand and drove south toward home.

Alone in the car, the heaviness my father had feared descended like a choking gas. Lightheartedness was not an option for me as it no doubt had not been for him. It was unimaginable that they were both gone. I pulled over at a rest stop, flung open the door, and gulped the air. This was how it felt to be an orphan — suffocating, adrift without oxygen.

I returned to the university administrative job, from which I had taken a leave of absence, and to Eric, the man I'd been living with and was considering marrying. I should have been happy to go home, to get my life back on its normal rhythm, but the truth was, I was viewing things through new eyes and everything now looked tarnished or broken. I no longer felt capable of the joy I once felt. I found myself picking fights with Eric; he irritated me even when the things he did and said were loving and selfless.

"My parents invited us for Thanksgiving," he said one night after dinner. "They'd love to see you, Helen."

Thanksgiving! I shuddered thinking of it. Mother's Day had been bad enough these last few years, but now that my father was gone, every holiday was going to be a torment. Eric's parents were big-hearted and boisterous, and had produced, besides Eric, four other children, some of whom had children of their own. Visiting them and their clan would be like stepping into an electric current. I dug my nails into my palms.

"I'm not ready for that," I said.

"Getting away would be good for you."

"Please, don't press me." I got up and cleared the table. "You should go by yourself."

"We're a couple. We should celebrate holidays together. Or are you trying to tell me something?"

"You can't imagine how I feel," I said.

"Of course I can. Having living parents doesn't make me a shallow person."

"Nothing has ever gone wrong for you."

"Not true at all. It seems that *you* have." It was so quiet I could hear the refrigerator motor. This was one step away from another conversation, one I dreaded. I began to cry.

He tried to take back his hurtful words, putting his arm around me and whispering, "What can I do to make you happy?"

"Just leave me alone, for now." I turned from his embrace and walked out of the room. All I wanted to do was sleep. No, all I wanted to do was to phone my parents and ask their advice. But they and their wisdom were gone while the world went on spinning. I wouldn't have blamed Eric if he'd had enough and asked me to leave, but I was too entombed in my sorrow to do or say the things it would take to turn it all around.

My friend Delia worked in Admissions, downstairs from my office in the Alumni Center. We often met for lunch. She was a good listener and liked to talk. She was divorced from Glenn, a physics professor at the college, who'd committed a fatal error with one of the graduate students in the economics department, but was still in love with Delia and wouldn't give up trying to get back together, even after three years apart. I had no idea how Delia really felt about him; it changed with each conversation. And although she joked about Glenn's showing up at her office at least two mornings a week with a bag of doughnuts and a container of coffee, she didn't discourage him.

She brought me one of her jelly doughnuts and pulled up a chair next to my desk.

"Eric's a good man, Helen. Don't blow it," Delia said.

"Sometimes I feel like I'm in a balloon, drifting over the earth with no way of landing. All that life down there — I can see it, but it's going on without me."

"It's just a matter of time before your re-entry," Delia said.

I told her about Thanksgiving — that I would be alone and that it was all my doing.

"Don't be too hard on yourself," she said.

Lemon filling squirted out the doughnut hole and plopped onto my skirt. I mopped it up with paper towels and some water left in a bottle I used for my window sill plants. I shrugged at the wet, sticky stain.

"Helen, I know you're grieving, and forgive me for saying this, but have you looked at yourself since you came back from New York? You're a real mess."

"I don't care how I look," I said.

"Maybe you'd feel better if you did."

Later, while washing my hands in the restroom down the hall, I glanced up and saw in the mirror what Delia meant. I looked like an unkempt ghost. The fluorescent light over the sink emphasized the pallor of my face and the plum-colored crescents under my eyes, which were blood-shot with lids pillowy from tears and lack of sleep. And how long had it been since I bothered with my hair, other than gathering it into a shaggy ponytail, where I wouldn't have to see it? I removed the rubber band and, pulling a brush from my purse, began to work away at the tangles. When I returned the brush, I noticed my mother's lipstick at the bottom of the bag. I lifted off the fluted metal casing and twisted the base to reveal the color. It was so very pink — a shade not unlike the droopy-headed peo-nies that had grown in my parents' garden — a pink that would look good, perhaps, only on blondes with fair complexions. My mother's coloring. I leaned forward, angled the still-beveled edge toward my upper lip, and carefully drew an arc, first on the right side and then on the left. When that was done, I blotted my lips together, checked my teeth for smears, and returned to my desk.

Within a few minutes, my lips began to tingle — as though tiny needle points were tapping out an irregular tattoo. I wondered if I was allergic to one of the components of the lipstick, but then, abruptly, the Morse code-like rhythm stopped, and I went back to concentrating on the next year's budget projections for alumni activities. As I sat there staring at the computer screen, my shoulders, arms, and even my fingers, scrolling through and editing the spreadsheets, became as relaxed as they'd be lying in a bath of warm water. Even more remarkable, I wanted desperately to see Eric, to try my hardest to connect with him again before he gave up on me.

I turned off the computer, sprinted to the car and sped home, not caring who saw me leave in mid-afternoon. When I arrived at the house, Eric was already there. It was his half-day at the pediatric clinic. I fumbled with the keys and when I finally burst in, Eric was standing over the kitchen sink eating his favorite snack — a bagel with banana and jelly. I pulled the sandwich out of his hand, dropped the gooey mess onto the counter, and began to cover his face with kisses.

"Wait," he said, laughing. "Let me swallow first."

I pulled back and said, "Well, make it fast."

We scooted out of the kitchen, taking off our clothing, dropping items here and there on our way to the bedroom. We continued laughing until we sank down onto the mattress and made love. It was a glorious way to end the day, and I hoped it would be the start of a new era for the two of us.

Eric napped for a while afterward. His face and neck were smeared with lipstick. I smiled at his sleeping form, closed the door to the bedroom and went out to the kitchen.

I thought about cooking dinner. I was famished. I opened one of the cookbooks I took from my parents' house and sat down at the table to find a recipe that included ingredients we had on hand. I flipped through the pages, one by one, looking at the photographs and the instructions. But then, as though a light burning too hot fizzled out abruptly, I no longer felt like it. A cold wave of melancholy washed over me and I wanted to get back into bed, but not with Eric. I couldn't stand the thought of him touching me again.

But then Eric came into the room, clean-faced and grinning. He said, "Let's go out for dinner. I feel like celebrating. Got my girl back!"

I knew I had to force myself to go. I couldn't disappoint him. Not now. So I nodded and left the room to get ready. I didn't deserve easy-going and forgiving Eric. For those qualities alone, I should have loved him unconditionally. But, I was falling back into a dark hole and I needed to climb out fast. I brushed my hair, sprayed my ankles with cologne and put on an outfit I knew Eric liked. And then, I glanced in the full-length mirror behind the bedroom door. I looked okay from the neck down, but my face seemed ashen and somehow out of focus as though I were fading before my eyes. I blinked and rooted around inside my purse until I found my mother's lipstick. I quickly slicked it on and, ignoring the prickling sensation, grabbed my coat and left with Eric.

"I want to go with you to your parents over Thanksgiving, if the invitation is still open," I said. We had just finished sharing an appetizer and were holding hands across the small bistro table.

"Helen, are you sure? The noise, the kids, the questions from everyone."

"You were right. It would do me good."

The entrees arrived, and we began to eat. The food was scrumptious, and we exchanged forkfuls and fed each other, laughing like teenagers. But as we came to the end of the meal, I began to feel uneasy. I excused myself and went to the ladies' room. I refreshed my lipstick, and in a few minutes, the anxious gloom departed.

⌒

"Helen, you need help. This is all in your mind," Delia said the next day over cups of coffee when I described to her in detail what I called the *lipstick phenomenon*. "I'll give you the name of someone I saw when Glenn was messing around with that slutty student. She's very good to talk to."

"This is not something a therapist, or anyone, could understand," I said. "There's no logic here. And I don't need someone to talk to. I have you."

"Well, as your friend I'm telling you that this isn't a normal reaction to a parent's death. Stop dwelling on it. Worry about someone else for a change."

"Like whom?" I said, but as soon as the words were out of my mouth I knew something was up with Delia. "What's wrong?" I asked.

Delia took a deep breath. "Glenn wants us to remarry."

"That's not news. The whole campus knows it." I took a sip of coffee, trying hard not to disturb my lipstick.

"Yes," she said. "But now I'm pregnant." She quickly added, "It happened seven weeks ago when I let Glenn stay over."

"That is so great!" I'd thought for a moment someone else was in the picture. "And you're going to say yes, have the baby, and live happily ever after. Right?"

"No, I'm not. I don't trust Glenn not to hurt me again."

"But do you still love him?"

"Well, that makes it worse, don't you think? The more I care, the deeper the pain."

"People make mistakes," I said. "And good people learn from them."

Delia's eyes squinted. "Funny, you're just about the last person who should be giving advice to couples. Next you'll be lending me your mother's lipstick. Anyway, the girl is still here, getting her degree. I'm sure there's still chemistry between those two."

"That girl will be gone once she has her degree. You and Glenn have

47

decades to build a new life out of that mistake." I wasn't trying to soothe Delia; I really meant it. "So what will you do?" I asked.

"I'm going to have the baby, but whether or not I'll keep it is still up in the air."

"You *have* told Glenn, haven't you?"

"No."

⁓

The trip to Eric's family in western Massachusetts turned out to be bliss-ful. The weather was crisp, and although all the leaves had fallen weeks before, the low-slung sun was strong, filling the countryside with brilliant shadows. We left home two days before the holiday in order to miss the traffic, and on the day before Thanksgiving, we hiked for hours in the hills near his parents' home. The darkness that had swaddled me released its hold and I felt as carefree as I ever had in my life. Eric's parents were wonderful — friendly and welcoming, but, at the same time, non-intru-sive. I began to think about the future.

On Thanksgiving Day, while all Eric's relatives sat around the large oak table in the dining room chatting, eating and drinking, my left hand played with the metal case of my mother's lipstick deep within the pocket of my skirt. These days, it never left my possession. During the soup course, I tried to guide the spoon into my mouth without touching my lips, but I must have appeared like a baby bird with its beak wide open before slamming it closed around the food, because everyone at the table, including the children, stared uneasily in my direction.

"Dear, do you have TMJ dysfunction? You look so uncomfortable," Eric's mother asked.

"Maybe, a little," I said. The condition sounded familiar, but I couldn't remember exactly what it was. "No, really, I'm fine."

So I settled on eating like a normal human being, but excused myself after every course to go to the bathroom to refresh my lipstick.

Eric and I slept on opposite sides of the house: he, in his old boyhood room, and I, in the guest bedroom. This arrangement worked out well since I was able to wash my face at night, not worrying about the how the demon that crept back into me through my bare lips would affect my feelings and behavior toward Eric.

⁓

Delia was less than encouraging when I barged into her office and described my weekend with Eric's family.

"A self-fulfilling prophesy," she said. "You believe bad things will happen if you don't wear the lipstick and then, by some bizarre means, you make them happen. You need to get a grip on reality."

"No, what I need is another identical lipstick. I'm running low," I said.

"And the company discontinued Rose Serenity a few years ago."

Delia covered her face with her hands and rubbed her eyes. "Try putting it on only one lip or, even better, put it where it won't come off when you eat — like under your arm."

"I tried that. It didn't work. It has to be on my mouth. It's like my words won't come out right if that color isn't on it."

Delia typed on her keyboard for a few minutes and then said, "I'm searching for an online site." She rotated the screen so that I could see. "There's the lipstick."

I studied the ad. The name was right, but the color looked wrong; it was too mauve-y and didn't have enough sparkle. The case wasn't fluted metal and the company that sold it was different from the original. "That's not it," I said.

"Well, buy it and pretend it is," she said.

"Delia, I'm not crazy."

"Then stop acting as though you are."

I looked at Delia and could see that she was frightened for me. Perhaps it was a mistake to have spilled it all out, especially since she had her own problems.

"Have you made any decisions about…you know…the baby?" I asked.

"No. I did tell Glenn and that was a huge mistake," she said.

"It's never a mistake to tell the truth. He loves you. And you love him. Why can't you forgive him?"

"I can forgive him, but it'll always be at the back of my mind that he'll cheat again. I just don't know if I want to live with that."

"What would it take to put it behind you?"

"I don't know," she said. "A sign? Isn't that what we're all looking for in some way?"

When I got back to my desk, I continued to search for the lipstick — using the words rose and serenity — for someplace that might have leftover stock. Other than what Delia came up with, I found a chat room where one woman posted an update on her quest for a state of tranquility by buying roses every week and scattering the petals around her bedroom, and another site that sold single note fragrance perfumes. I even checked out the cosmetics company to see if they'd substituted another name for the same color, but nothing came of that either. All records of that lipstick had disappeared, as though it had never existed. Like my mother. Gone.

I took a walk at lunchtime to think things through. Without the lipstick, I was a bear — impossible to get along with; depressed, unsociable, and grudging. But was that true? Delia got along with me. And actually, so did almost everyone. Except Eric. The thought that I would forever need a tool to love or even tolerate Eric filled me with alarm.

I stopped in at the university library, one of my favorite places. It had a music room where students could check out CDs and listen on their headphones while studying in private carrels. It was one of those places where you could get transported out of your current world and into a different time, and it was my secret spot on campus. I came here when things all around me were going haywire. But today, I was here to use the restroom. As I was washing up, I saw a young woman at the next sink putting on makeup. She didn't look like one of the undergraduates; she was in her mid-twenties, stylishly dressed in a short clingy skirt, patterned black tights, and a gold necklace that said *Andrea*. She took her time, as would an artist contemplating a canvas, meticulously puffing powder on her nose and brow using a large, soft brush. Something about her seemed familiar, but I didn't think we'd ever met. Then, she began to apply lipstick and, for a moment, I held my breath as adrenaline coursed through my veins. I recognized the fluted metal casing and the color she was dabbing on was a deep iridescent pink.

"Where did you get that lipstick?" I blurted out.

The woman stopped and stared at me as though I had accused her of stealing. I knew right away it was the wrong tone to have taken. I should have said how much I liked the color and did she know where I could buy one like it. But it was too late.

"What's it to you?" she said. She put everything back in a zippered bag and then tossed it into a large tote.

"Listen," I said. "I'll buy that lipstick from you. Name a price."

"That's disgusting," she said and left the ladies room.

⤎

The frosty air suffused my lungs, urging me to walk on. I was too agitated to return to my office, but I couldn't think of where else to go. On the path, in the distance, an elderly couple bundled in parkas was strolling hand in hand. The man, who had been talking to his companion, shifted his gaze in my direction and then lifted his hand as if in greeting. I stopped walking, squinted, and then rubbed my eyes. I didn't believe in the impossible, and yet, somehow, I always knew they would return. Because I still needed them. Because there was unfinished business in my life. Because I was clutching the lipstick. I ran toward them as fast as I could in my narrow skirt and heels.

But as I closed in on the couple, I saw the woman's dark curly hair and the man's beard and moustache. They were in their forties, and on this cold afternoon were most likely cutting across the campus to get to the other side of town. I stepped aside to let them pass. The man said, "Nice day," and resumed the conversation with his companion.

I approached the quadrangle that housed the science laboratories and I knew what I had to do. It was an experiment to prove something crucial to myself, that I could be a selfless person — as worthy as my parents had been, but without their help. I reached into my jacket pocket, found a tissue and rubbed the color off my lips.

By the time I arrived at the physics building, I was out of breath. I lumbered up the front steps and barged into Glenn's lab, a place I had been only once, years ago, when I came with Delia to bring Glenn supper during one of his marathon experiments.

"Helen! What a nice surprise," he said. "What brings you here?"

I looked around and saw that we weren't alone. Two technicians were setting up electronic equipment and a young student sat at a high bench copying numbers into a bound notebook.

"Is there somewhere we can talk privately?" I asked.

"This sounds serious. Are you okay?"

"Please Glenn — it's about Delia…and you."

"Sure," he said. "My office is down the hall."

Glenn found a chair for me and sat behind his desk. He moved an apple that must have been sitting there for months; the brick-colored skin was badly puckered and I wondered why he hadn't tossed it in the garbage. I didn't have to go through the preliminaries. In fact, he started the conversation.

"Is there any way you can help me with Delia?" he asked.

Glenn was disheveled. His sandy hair stood up in small peaks on the top of his head and his shirt was only half tucked into his chinos. One eyeglass temple piece was held together with what seemed to be black electrical tape. He hardly looked like a lothario. He looked sheepish and sweet.

"Tell me why you betrayed her," I said. Glenn stared at the apple for a moment, and when he finally looked in my direction, his eyes were filmy with tears.

"It was a terrible mistake. The worst I've ever made. I've tried to atone in every way I know how, but it seems it's not enough."

"But why did you do it?"

"There's no excuse for what I did, but it was the only time in my life that someone pursued me. Even with Delia, I had to beg her to marry me, and when she said yes, I had the feeling that although she loved me it was more of a deep trust and friendship than a physical attraction. You see this apple?" He pointed to the desiccated fruit on his desk. "That's me. Who would choose it when there are other juicy specimens available? With Andrea, it was she who was the aggressor — teasing and touching me endlessly. She said I turned her on. She said she had to have me. I

51

didn't really want her, but I did want someone who wanted me that way."

I sat silent for a moment. Andrea. The girl in the bathroom. No wonder she'd looked familiar. Delia had pointed her out to me once through a window in the admissions office.

"But that's all over. I swear to you, it'll never happen again."

"It's not me you have to swear to," I said.

"I could talk my lungs out and Delia won't change her mind about me." He got up and paced around the office. "You're her friend. Tell me, do I have any chance at all? I want to be her husband again and to be a father to our baby."

"She wants a sign," I said.

"A sign? What kind of a sign?"

"You'll have to figure that one out," I said. "But it's got to have meaning for her, something that will make her trust you again."

"Okay. I'll do it. I'll do anything. A sign. Jeez!" He looked as though someone handed him an incomprehensible physics problem. "But when I come up with it, can I call on you if I need help?" he asked.

"Absolutely! I'm rooting for you both."

"You're a good friend, Helen. I hope things are going well for you."

And with that, I left.

⌒

I stood on the steps outside the physics labs and slipped on my gloves. The smell of snow was in the air and I could imagine a blizzard descending from the north in a day or two. I walked back to my office building, got in my car and sat there as it warmed up. I had no idea what kind of a sign Glenn would come up with, but he was smart and driven by his deepest desires. It might be a literal sign — a poster, or an ad in the local paper, or even more flamboyant, skywriting saying, "Come back. I will treasure you always." Or it might be a gesture — a volume of love poetry, or a book of baby names. Whatever the sign, I had no doubt that eventually they would end up where they belonged: in each other's lives.

I drove back home and immediately went through the house gathering my belongings. I found a large suitcase and some moving boxes in the basement and began to pack. Then, I called Delia to ask if I could stay with her for a week or two until I found a place of my own.

"You're really leaving?" she said.

"It was what you said about each of us looking for a sign. I had one of my own for weeks, but I didn't see it," I said.

"Your mother's lipstick," she said.

"It made me see I wasn't right for Eric. And he wasn't right for me."

"He'll be blown away," Delia said.

"At first, maybe. But in the long run, he'll find someone who adores him. He deserves no less."

I loaded the car with as much as could fit. I considered junking the blue suede heels and then decided to keep them just in case they, too, had a message. I tossed the lipstick into the garbage and went back into the house to wait for Eric — to have the conversation we should have had a long time ago.

Office Visit

Wandajune Bishop-Towle

I'D LIKE TO TALK TO YOU. The doctor shouts. LEEEeeeeww, li li LIKE! my stepson echoes. He's autistic, not deaf, I say. David's aides are with us, two men the size of bodyguards. As is David, at twenty. The aides give each other a look — they've seen these doctor-parent face-offs before. But I'm a new stepmother, not just Dad's girlfriend now, and this is my first doctor's appointment with him. I answer questions.

No, he's never been married.

No, no girlfriend.

No, no beers on the weekend.

Yes. I have his list of medications here — Keppra, for seizures; Luvox, seems to help with his obsessions. Such as? Whales, dolphins, sharks. He carries around a picture of a Great White breaching. David, show us your picture. With the reverence of a curator, David slides from his pocket the magazine page, folded and unfolded many times. He holds it up for us: Leviathan, flung against the sky. SHARK! he says. The doctor nods.

WHERE DOES IT HURT? David lifts his shirt up, and studies his belly, rapt. His attention often snags on details the rest of us just pass over — the way a drop of water grows before it falls from a faucet, his curved reflection on the back of a spoon. Maybe it's a mole that mesmerizes him.

TAKE EVERYTHING OFF. David stands, obedient, while his aides unbutton, one on the shirt placket; the other, the cuffs. He undoes his pants himself, which fall into a heap on the floor, steps out first one foot, then the other. He hesitates a moment, then turns away from me to take off his underwear. The men hold open the gown. David stretches forth his arms to meet the sleeves. They steady him as he climbs onto the exam table. The paper crinkles and tears a bit.

David leans back, propped on his elbows, and looks at — me. He doesn't want to lay down. *It's OK Sweetheart,* I tell him, *it's OK.* Each man eases down a shoulder as David rolls back slowly, keeping me in his gaze.

Old Habits

Liz Drayer

The sliding doors parted, and Grapefruit shuffled through. Gayle watched the old man make his way down the main aisle of Home Stuff and take a right into Plumbing. She glanced at the clock. Nine A.M. Grapefruit was nothing if not punctual.

A tug on Gayle's apron made her whirl. "Your boyfriend's here," said Ken, nodding at the old man.

"Very funny," said Gayle.

Ken grabbed a bottle of spray cleaner and wiped down Gayle's register belt. Could he actually be jealous of the old man who came through her line every day? The thought made Gayle smile. When she'd started at the store and couldn't tell a wrench from a buzz saw, Ken Dugan had showed her around, patiently answering questions she was sure sounded idiotic, though she wasn't his trainee and had only been hired as a cashier. But, Gayle had a feeling those "self-checkout" lines could make her job obsolete in no time and wanted to learn as much about the store as she could. Ken knew the place down to the last toilet flapper.

But judging by Mrs. Dugan's nasty looks when she came to pick up her husband, Ken must have mentioned Gayle's name, maybe a little too often. Not that she'd encouraged him or flirted. What was she supposed to do when he was friendly, snub him? Of course no wife wanted her husband chasing a twenty-year-old. But come on! Did Mrs. D. really think Gayle was after pot-bellied Ken? He was sweet, but old enough to be her father and then some.

Ken tapped the face of his watch. "Give Grapefruit five minutes to pick up some random junk, and he'll come crutching up to your register like he does every day."

Gayle shrugged. "So what? He's lonely, or bored, and likes to talk." The old man's real name was Stan, short for Stanislaus, but Ken said his head looked like the grapefruit you saw bumping down I-4 in huge trucks, round but flattened in places with patches of red and brown. Somehow, the name had stuck.

Ken bumped Gayle with his hip. "Lighten up. I don't call him names to his face, do I? But it's cute how you stick up for him." He winked and moved off to help a woman struggling with an armful of shelf brackets.

What would Ken say if he knew Grapefruit called her every afternoon when she got off from work, Gayle wondered. He'd even sent her a birthday card a few weeks ago. They'd started off talking about baseball, how the Rays' bullpen stunk this year, how their star player was way overpaid. Then, he told her about growing up in Poland, coming to Florida and marrying an American girl, who happened to be Gayle's double, or at least she was sixty years ago. Gayle liked talking to the old man; he was sort of grandfatherly. She figured this was what people did with grandfathers — talked about sports, listened to them tell stories about the old days.

In the next lane, a lone customer fumbled with the self-checkout, and Gayle helped her ring up her Spackle and Gorilla Glue. She liked how the shoppers were grateful for any help, as if they were surprised that she actually knew something. That was the good and bad part about being young, she figured; no one expected much of you, but they might not give you a chance to prove yourself either. And she wanted to do a good job at Home Stuff, maybe move up from cashier to one of the departments. She could picture herself in Windows, for example, helping customers choose Roman shades and vertical blinds. She'd never had a place of her own to decorate and was full of ideas.

Back at her register, she counted the change in her drawer for the third time that morning, one eye on the big front doors of the store, which was really a warehouse that smelled like her shop class in middle school. The morning had been quiet so far, not the usual rush of over-all-clad workmen grabbing supplies for their jobs. And where was Dean? The hunky roofer came in every day for something or other. Gayle hoped his visits were really an excuse to see her, not that Dean ever said much when he came through her line. She knew his name from his credit card, but they'd never actually conversed beyond "Hi" and "Thanks" and "Did you find everything okay?" She hoped he was working up the nerve to ask her for a date. How long that might take she couldn't be sure.

As Ken had predicted at five minutes past nine, Grapefruit emerged from Hardware and made his slow way toward Gayle's register. He watched the floor, as if some obstacle might pop up and trip him. Despite his slight shuffle, the old guy had plenty of kick left in him; the week before she'd seen him jump out of the way when a shelf full of two by fours crashed to the floor. He moved pretty fast when he needed to.

He smiled as he reached her register and raised one hand in greeting, the other clutching some picture wire and a four pack of bulbs. The old man wasn't much taller than Gayle and smelled faintly medicinal, which for some reason she found soothing. As he laid the items on her belt, Dean emerged from Lumber pushing a cart full of fascia board. He steered into line behind Grapefruit and grinned at the floor.

Gayle's stomach plummeted. Where had *he* come from? She didn't even have time now to fix her makeup. She smoothed the curls back from her face with a gesture she hoped looked alluring and wondered how he'd entered the store without her noticing. Maybe he'd sneaked in through Garden, which had its own entrance.

Just be cool and don't drop anything, she told herself as she hurried to ring up Grapefruit's stuff. The old man stepped aside and motioned to Dean to take his place in line. No! Gayle wanted to yell. He needs time to work up courage to talk to me. Don't ruin his rhythm.

But Dean shook his head at Grapefruit. "Oh no, sir, you were first, and you only have two items anyway." Gayle couldn't help grinning. He was nice to old people — big points for that. Or maybe he wanted to talk to her uninterrupted. Even better.

"How did you enjoy the game last night?" Grapefruit said in his heavy accent. He reached a trembling hand into his billfold and pulled out a twenty.

"Just fine!" She returned his change and handed over his items in a bag. Please, don't start analyzing last night's blown save. I have important business with the next customer in line.

Grapefruit pointed at his watch. "Two o'clock, first game of the Toronto series."

"You make sure we win, okay?" Gayle looked over at Dean. Next!

"I can take you over here," Ken called from the next register and motioned Dean into his line. No, this couldn't be happening, Gayle thought, as Dean and his cart moved to Ken's register. Dean glanced back at her with a look she hoped was disappointment.

She shook her head as she watched Grapefruit place his bag in a cart.

"Sorry if I held up your line," he said, grinning. Gayle stared. Had he purposely tried to stop her from waiting on Dean? That couldn't be. Grandfathers didn't wreck your romances. Not that she knew much about grandfathers, or fathers for that matter, having no experience with either. Even her mom had given Gayle away to a friend when she was eight. The friend got tired of her too, and the series of foster homes that followed ensured she'd never have family in the usual sense of the word. Just some nice, and not so nice, caretakers to feed and clothe her for a while.

She watched Grapefruit exit the store and cross the parking lot. Ken's voice boomed from the next register where he was ringing up Dean. "You working some big job? I've seen you in here every day this week."

"Putting a roof on a five thousand square foot place up in East Lake." Dean wore a blue plaid shirt with the sleeves rolled up, revealing gold hair on his powerful arms. Gayle tried not to stare.

"Weather guy says it'll hit ninety the rest of the week."

"Yikes," said Dean. He swiped his card and signed the screen. Transaction complete, he and his fascia rolled out the door.

Gayle sighed. At this rate, they'd never get past the "have a nice day" stage. Maybe if she were working out on the floor...

Reality intruded in the form of two flats of begonias which rolled towards her register. A woman held a credit card out, and Gayle realized she'd been so focused on Ken and Dean, she had no idea how long the woman had been there.

"Sorry," Gayle mumbled, and placed the begonias in her wagon, taking care not to crush any blooms.

"Do you have some brown paper I can put in my trunk so it doesn't get dirty?" the woman asked.

"They have that over in Garden." Gayle hated when she couldn't give customers everything they needed. Why didn't Garden ring up their own people? If she ran the store, that's how it would be. Now her register belt was grimy from the flowers and dirt.

For the rest of the morning, shoppers moved steadily through Gayle's line. At noon, she brought her bag lunch to the picnic tables behind the store which the manager, Mr. Chu, had set up for the staff. A striped umbrella shaded each table, not a bad place to eat at all. She liked Mr. Chu, who always smiled at her when he walked the floor, and never made her feel stupid for asking questions. Maybe she'd mention the problems with Garden to him.

Ken patted the seat next to him and moved over to make room for Gayle. "Your boyfriend ask for your phone number yet?" he asked as she slid in beside him.

Gayle started. Was her crush on Dean that obvious? "How did you know — " she began, then realized Ken was talking about Grapefruit. "Actually, I gave him my number the first day he came through my line."

"That was a bad idea, hon."

Gayle shrugged. "He calls once in awhile." Okay, every day, but Ken didn't need all the details. "We both like baseball. He saw Don Drysdale pitch in the World Series."

"Is that so?" Ken took a huge bite of his sandwich. "How does his wife feel about your little chats?"

"She died a long time ago." Ken smirked at the other guys at the table. "We're just friends, you know."

"Right," said Ken. "And I'm Justin Bieber."

"I'm just being nice to an old man."

"He doesn't think you're just a friend. He's got ideas in his head you don't want to know about, trust me."

Eeew, thought Gayle. She didn't believe it. Sometimes Ken thought he knew everything about everything, but she was sure this time he was mistaken.

Ken crumpled the foil from his sandwich and stuffed it in a bag. "Don't be surprised if he pulls out an engagement ring next time he comes through your line."

"I'm just being friendly. It doesn't mean anything."

"Have it your way." Ken and the guys headed back to the floor, leaving Gayle to finish lunch alone. Maybe she'd been wrong to give Grapefruit her number. He didn't like her "that way," did he?

The store got busy that afternoon and five o'clock came quickly. Glad to be free, Gayle pulled off her apron and stuffed it in her purse. But before she could head out the door, a small woman appeared at her register, dark lipstick bleeding beyond the thin line of her mouth.

"Sorry, I'm closed," Gayle said, in a voice she hoped sounded firm but polite. The woman's frown lines deepened.

"I'm not here to buy anything. My father does plenty of buying already."

"I don't understand."

"Stan. You know, your best pal."

"Stan — is your father?"

The woman's eyes narrowed. "Do you let all the customers call you on the phone? Or just the ones you want money from? He spends hundreds on junk he doesn't need, coming in here to 'visit.' What's your game, honey?"

"Grapefr — Stan and I are just friends!"

"You've got lots of old men friends, I bet. He's not rich, you know."

"I don't want money. You've got this all wrong."

The woman leaned close to Gayle's face, and Gayle took a step back. Shoppers were stopping to stare.

"I can't stop him from coming here," the woman said. "But I blocked your number from his phone. Party's over, sweetie."

"Is there a problem?" Mr. Chu hurried toward them, black hair falling over his eyes. Gayle had never been so glad to see him.

The woman poked a finger at Gayle. "This girl's taking money from my father. What are you going to do about it?"

"That's not true!" said Gayle. "He never gave me anything." Gayle remembered Ken's engagement ring crack and shivered.

"Don't lie. He sent you a hundred dollars!"

"I don't know what you're talking about."

"The check came back to the house because the address was wrong. That's how I found it. I asked him who you were, and he said 'a nice girl who's all alone.' Is that what you tell all your patsies?"

"I — don't have a family. I may have mentioned that." A crowd of customers had gathered now, no longer interested in the barbeque grills and mosquito zappers.

"Let's take this to my office," Mr. Chu said, and led the way to the back of the store. Twenty minutes later they emerged, Grapefruit's daughter with a Home Stuff gift card, Gayle with a lecture on boundaries and the appearance of impropriety. Mr. Chu said he was sure she'd use better judgment next time and wished her luck. But he had to let her go.

Just a few belongings remained in her locker, and Gayle retrieved them and headed towards the store exit. The lamps in Lighting gave off a dim glow. She'd never been fired before, and what was worse, she'd done nothing wrong. It was so unfair! Maybe she didn't realize how her actions appeared to others, like Mr. Chu said. But why were appearances so important? She'd had no bad intentions. Now she'd lost the first real job she'd ever had. It was time to move on, again, like she'd moved on from every house, every school, every family. She thought Home Stuff might be a place where she could belong, more than a stop on the way to somewhere else. But she'd been wrong.

As she neared the store exit, the doors parted and Mrs. Dugan appeared. Probably picking Ken up for their Friday dinner at the son's, Gayle thought. She nodded at Gayle and continued down the aisle. Mrs. D. might like her better if she were ugly, she thought. If she were ugly she'd probably still have her job. Things hadn't changed much since high school, where every girl wanted to be queen. Women pretended they were part of some sisterhood, but that wasn't how things were at all.

She hurried out the door so none of her coworkers would try to catch up with her. They'd hear the whole crummy story soon enough.

In front of Garden, vehicles lined the curb. Shoppers loaded in purchases — topsoil, stones for edging plant beds, bags of mulch. People were constantly buying this mulch stuff, and Gayle had no idea why. Couldn't they find wood chips on the ground for free? Shoppers darted in and out of the traffic, creating a dangerous mix of cars and bodies.

Gayle stepped off the curb between two trucks when one began backing up. She jumped back onto the sidewalk. Another second and that truck would have flattened me, she thought. She sank down on a bench, shaking, and put her head in her hands.

"You okay?" said a familiar voice. Gayle looked up and saw Dean.

"I'm fine, thanks."

"I almost backed right over you. You scared the heck out of me. Good thing I saw you in time." He sat down next to her.

"Weren't you just here this morning?"

"I stopped back after work. For some plants and stuff, so I could work on my yard this weekend. I need more mulch to keep down the weeds." He grinned. "And I hoped I'd get lucky and run into *you*. We kind of got interrupted this morning." He nodded at the restaurant across the street. "That place, Bubba's, makes great pretzel burgers. We should celebrate that I didn't run over you."

"Sure," Gayle said. She felt hungry now, starved. She slung her tote over her shoulder and followed Dean across the parking lot.

One of Them Little Buggers

Brian Kamsoke

Darren stood in the doorway looking at an empty crib, alongside an empty dresser, and considered the consequences of what he was about to say. "What if," he said, "we went right to in vitro?"

Peggy busied herself smoothing out a final strip of wallpaper then turned toward Darren with what he'd expected — a curious expression. "Are you saying you want to skip the IUIs?"

"I'm not saying that," he said. "But how many IUIs do we have remaining?"

"One more after tomorrow."

"And then the last step is in vitro."

They'd been seeing a fertility doctor for two years now, and every morning for those two years Peggy woke and before getting out of bed took her temperature and recorded the results on a chart — hormonal activity dictating their sex life. Despite their best efforts, every month her period came on time with the exception of one month when she was four days late. If it is true a pregnant woman has a certain glow about her, then Darren thought Peggy had that glow for those four days. But the period eventually came, and the glow, if there was one, dissipated.

"I'm thinking the stress of trying to have a child is becoming a problem," he said.

"So you want to stop trying?"

"I'm saying the doctor said stress could cause infertility. So I'm just saying we try in vitro and if it doesn't work then…"

"Then what?"

"Then we'll know."

Peggy tucked the remaining roll of unused wallpaper under her arm while carefully balancing a pan of water in her hands. "I need to cleanup before dinner. Are you going hunting?"

"Just for a while," and he stepped into the hallway allowing Peggy to pass. He admired her walk down the hallway, a waddle mostly, never particularly graceful, even clumsy, but still alluring. Such a tiny body. He often marveled at the thought of her giving birth.

Darren stepped into the bathroom, and after using the toilet and washing his hands, he stood for a moment staring at his reflection in the mirror. His reflection — it appeared as though behind a thin, gray film like the mirror had somehow fogged over. He wiped the mirror with the sleeve of his shirt and determined it must be the lighting because the fogginess didn't clear. Leaning over the sink, staring through the foggy haze at his appearance, he frowned. He hated his face, always had. The corner of his lower lip hung down as though snagged by a fishhook. He'd been born two months premature and became stuck in the birthing canal, so the doctor used forceps to pry him out but had squeezed too tight, compressing Darren's skull, leaving an indentation and destroying the nerves in Darren's lower lip. His parents said he was lucky to be born. His mother had had two previous miscarriages. Still, he hated his face and grew a beard as soon as he could to conceal the damage. He brushed his hand over his beard. Some of the whiskers had turned white. Too early, he thought, for a man of thirty-one.

✑

Darren sat in his tree stand, a rifle butt wedged against his right shoulder, his finger on the trigger, the barrel balanced across his palm, a doe standing perfectly still for a center shot to the heart. An icy breeze brushed his cheek. Bands of sunlight broke through the gray forest. The sudden glare off freshly fallen snow stabbed at his eyes. He squinted. His heart thumped heavier. He drew a deep, chilly breath and held it. He felt himself rocking in the breeze. The doe turned. The rifle butt jolted his shoulder as the crack from the combustion blast echoed in the meadow. The doe bounded over a fallen tree and disappeared down a bank.

Cursing himself, he slung his rifle over his shoulder and scurried down his tree stand. He reached the spot where the doe had stood, saw droplets of blood in the snow, and began following the trail along the ridge. Blood droplets were spaced almost evenly between the hoof marks. He cursed himself again. He had missed his shot at the heart or lungs. He might have hit her in the belly, and that wasn't good. With a belly shot, she could survive through the night or even a couple days. He knew where she was going, though. She would make her way to the pond, leaving state land to cross onto Brannon's property, the eighty acres of woodland and meadows that dwarfed Darren's three-acre plot of land.

The trail turned down from the ridge into a darkened forest of hemlocks where "No Trespassing" signs had been nailed to tree trunks. With daylight creeping away, Darren considered his options. Dragging the doe's carcass, he'd never make it back up the ridge by nightfall. That was if he even located her before nightfall, and if she wasn't dead, it would take another shot to put her down. He didn't have any rope to hang the carcass from a tree to prevent coyotes from getting it. Again, he cursed himself for taking the shot he shouldn't have taken. But nothing could be done now. Best to leave her alone, let her lie down, let the bullet settle in and drain her strength. If he kept tracking her, she would keep running out of fear and instinct. But if he left her alone, eventually she'd lie down and wouldn't be able to get back up. He'd find her in the morning, close by, he hoped.

Darren began backtracking on his trail. The sound of snow crunching under his boots — the only sound he heard. The breeze had changed direction, the air now bloated with moisture. He knew what that meant. A lake effect snowstorm was building. Fresh snowfall would make it difficult, if not impossible, to track his doe. Before returning to the forest, Darren stood on the ridge peering west. The sun hung like a dirty snowball behind a flat mat of clouds stretched across the horizon. He held his bare hand, fingers outstretched, to the fading sunlight and noted how the light passed right through his palm. Strange. In fact, he could see blood vessels and capillaries and the bone structure as though his hand had been captured in an x-ray. He made a fist and spread his fingers again, but by this time, the light had escaped over the horizon and what he saw, or thought he saw, had disappeared with it.

They had been in this room before, in this position, alone, with Darren lying on the examination table, his boxers pulled down to his knees and Peggy standing over him stroking his erection. He kept his eyes closed, tried to concentrate, tried to ignore the voices in the hallway. "I'm coming," he said, and Peggy directed his penis into a sterile container. When the spasms passed and he'd emptied himself, Peggy capped the container and handed Darren a tissue.

"Good job," she said, and pinched his butt cheek.

Darren smiled. "My pleasure." He pulled on his pants and slipped on his boots. They walked down the hall and gave the container to the nurse at the counter. She then directed them to another room where Peggy removed her clothes and covered herself in a white smock. She sat on the examination table and Darren sat in a chair next to her.

After a long silence, Darren said, "How do I look to you?" Peggy flashed a curious smile. "Do I look the same to you?"

She reached and held his hand, her tone now more flirtatious, "As cute as ever," she said. "If the gray in your beard bothers you, it makes you look distinguished."

He wanted to elaborate, but the doctor entered — a tall Swede with thick blond hair and blue eyes. He carried a catheter attached to a syringe. "Everything looks good," he said. "The sperm count is great."

Darren felt both pride and relief, but noticed a certain agitation in his wife. "We have good vibes about it this time," he said.

The doctor, whose name was Eric, seemed to ignore the comment. Darren liked the doctor well enough, a fondness born of respect and envy; he respected him in the professional sense anyone would respect a doctor, yet he envied his intelligence, his suspected wealth, and even his physical stature — tall and lean with an athletic grace.

Peggy lay on her back with her knees in the air. The doctor parted her legs and guided the syringe inside her. Darren held her hand as the doctor forced the plunger forward, emptying the contents of the syringe. He then slowly withdrew the instrument. "That's it," he said.

"Good job, dear," Darren said, patting her hand.

Peggy remained on her back as directed by the doctor. "Continue doing what you're doing," he said. "Everything looks good. You're ovulating. The sperm count is good. You know, go home and…uh, you know… still have sex."

Darren wanted the doctor to know that he was still doing his part. "Yeah," he said, "we've been doing that." He smiled at Peggy, who blushed slightly.

The doctor scribbled something into a file folder and slapped the folder closed. "Sperm can survive a couple days," he said. "All we need to do is get one of them…uh, little buggers to the egg. And, you know, the more the better. One of them will beat out the others eventually. So, rest there for five minutes and then you're free to go."

After the doctor left the room, they sat in silence again. Darren stared at his hands and Peggy stared at the ceiling. Peggy began, "Isn't it odd he seems so timid talking about sex? I mean, for a fertility doctor?"

Darren agreed. Although he never admitted this to Peggy, he sometimes wondered what happened to the sterile container holding his sperm after they handed it to the nurse. He'd read one time of a fertility doctor substituting his own sperm during treatment. Paranoid perhaps. But who would ever know?

"What are you thinking?" she said.

Darren said, "If we make it back in time, I want to go out and track the doe before nightfall."

"Oh."

"What?"

"Nothing."

"I just feel bad. I never should have taken that shot. I don't want her suffering."

At a stoplight on the way home, Darren scooted forward to glance at his reflection in the rear-view mirror; it appeared translucent wherein he saw the traffic behind them merged into his reflection as though it was all one image. He sat back, adjusted his seat, and, when the light turned green, pressed lightly on the accelerator. "I think I might need glasses," he said.

"Is that why you missed the doe?"

Darren shot a glance at her, surprised by the sudden anger he felt. Trying to cap it, he said, carefully, "I'm just concerned the doe might have crossed onto Brannon's property."

Peggy stared out the side window. "What?"

"Brannon's. I might have to cross his land."

"Will you call first?"

"He'll never know." Darren had no intention of asking Brannon whether he could track the doe across his property. He disliked Brannon and his three boys, all of whom acted as if the state forest that abutted their property belonged to them.

"So, you're thinking the home equity?" Peggy said.

"What?"

"For in vitro?"

"That's what I was thinking."

"That's a lot of money."

"I know." He glanced again at her and saw her staring at him. "It's worth it, right? To try it. And then we'll know."

"And what if it doesn't work?"

Darren gained speed to pass the car ahead. "Then we'll just move on with our life. But at least we'll know."

Peggy returned her gaze out the side window. "Well, let's just see if this works first."

"That's what I mean. I'm just saying if it doesn't."

"I'm hungry. Let's stop somewhere and eat."

Darren checked the clock on the dashboard. Stopping somewhere would mean less daylight when they arrived home. Nevertheless, he pulled into a McDonald's drive-thru.

⁓

Just as Darren feared, freshly fallen snow had covered the doe's tracks. Under a heavy gray sky, he started down the ridge where he remembered the tracks leading. When he reached the pond, he scanned the shoreline in hopes of spotting the doe. If she were anywhere, she'd most likely be near the spillway where the current kept the ice thin, forming tiny pools of water.

Darren followed the shoreline in hopes of finding evidence of his doe. He knew Peggy was upset with him for leaving the cabin right after they arrived home. But she didn't understand. This doe was his responsibility. He shot her, wounded her because of taking a piss-poor shot, and now maybe she was suffering because of him. If she were still alive, he needed to find her and put her down. He'd drag her home, skin the hide, and cut up the meat. There'd be enough venison to last into the summer. Her death would not be in vain, her carcass not left to scavenging coyotes.

Snowdrifts snaked across the icy pond blown by a cold northwest wind. As Darren adjusted the rifle strap on his shoulder, movement on the far side of the pond caught his attention. Squinting through his binoculars, he saw only a dark stand of hemlocks sheltering the shoreline. He thought his doe might be hiding there. It would take thirty minutes,

Darren estimated, for him to trudge through the snow around the pond to reach the other side. With the butt of his rifle, he tapped the ice along the shore. It would take only a few minutes to walk across the pond. That would give him more time to drag the doe home before dark if, indeed, she was hiding amongst the hemlocks.

Darren took a couple cautionary steps. He kicked the ice with the heel of his boot. It felt solid, so he started across. Halfway, Darren heard more clearly now water rushing over the spillway, more powerful than he'd suspected. Then, the heel of his left boot slipped into a hole; stinging cold water quickly filled his boot. His first thought was how uncomfortable it would be to hike home with a wet boot and sock. Then he fell backwards. A slab of ice lifted behind him, and he slid into the water as easily as a child down a slide. His head went under. Water gurgled in his ears. The rifle strap slipped from his shoulder. He came to the surface gasping; the air burned his lungs. His clothes clung to him as though sucked inward. The water, like icy lances, penetrated him. He cursed himself for not realizing the ice was thinner out here in the middle of the pond where the current moved toward the spillway. He stretched his arms flat over the ice and rested his chin on the broken edge. The current swept his legs and torso under the ice sheet. He clumsily removed his gloves and dug his fingernails into the ice. He couldn't see the shoreline, only the tips of hemlock trees and above these the ridge that would lead him home.

The strength of the current moving under the ice surprised him. With one hand, he reached under the water to the knife on his belt. He unsnapped the holster and brought the knife to the surface. Holding the edge of the blade with his teeth, he twisted the handle to fully open the blade. His fingers began to cramp. He could barely feel the knife handle in his palm but was able to flip the knife around and stab the blade into the ice. He kicked with his feet and pulled on the knife for leverage. His shoulders lifted out of the water as he bent forward over the ice slab. He kicked harder, trying to lift his torso onto the slab when the ice cracked and shattered under him. He slipped back beneath the water. Surfacing, a broken slab of ice bounced off his cheek and floated in front of his eyes. He was still alive! His coat felt incredibly heavy. He swam against the current to the opposite side of the watery hole. He stabbed the ice with the knife, and, clawing with his other hand, gained leverage. The fast moving current lifted his legs to the surface, making it easier for him to crawl out of the watery hole and onto the ice.

He lay there for a few seconds afraid any movement might cause the ice to crack and dump him into the water again. A sudden hot wave of energy washed through him as he realized how close he'd come to dying, but then, like a candle flame snuffed by a breeze, he felt the cold air suck heat from his body. On his hands and knees to keep his weight evenly distributed, he crawled across the ice to the shoreline opposite to where he started across the pond. Reaching solid ground, he stood and leaned against a hemlock and stared back at the watery hole that appeared as a dark, gaping wound in an otherwise pristine snowy, woodland setting.

He had to think quickly. He hadn't much time. Already his clothes felt stiff and brittle from freezing. Icicles formed in his beard. His limbs ached. His eyes burned. He shook his arms and stomped his feet to get blood moving. Brannon's farmhouse — that was the closest house, nearer than his own. Darren turned from the pond and started through the forest in the direction he believed would lead him to Brannon's farmhouse. Along the way, his thoughts were of Peggy. His greatest fear was dying and leaving her alone.

The sun had set, and the remaining light hung in the snow-covered trees like an icy haze. Darren moved as swiftly as possible, attempting to jog, but his strides came awkward. He stumbled and the toe of his boot lodged into something that felt like packed mud. He tumbled forward, rolled, and, sitting up, found himself looking into the dead eyes of his doe. Unsure at first, he touched his bare hand to the doe's neck and felt her coarse hide, the coldness of her body. He located where he'd shot her. In the belly, just where he'd thought. Then he noticed another gunshot wound at the base of her skull. Somebody had found her before he had.

Exhausted, he rested his head momentarily against the doe's back, but he couldn't allow himself to sleep. He raised his head and saw twenty feet from him a fawn, its white speckled haunches clearly visible even in the dull light of dusk. The fawn's black nose sniffed the air. She stared at Darren, her head bowed as if to hide herself.

Darren stared back. The fawn did not move. He tried to gather his thoughts, concentrate. He hadn't seen a fawn when he took his shot. He wouldn't have pulled the trigger if he'd seen a fawn. A doe having a fawn this late in the year was unusual, but not impossible. He forced himself to his feet, but still the fawn refused to flee. Darren smelled pine smoke, and the thought of a nearby fire renewed his energy. He was close to Brannon's farmhouse.

Brannon's yellow porch light glowed in the clearing ahead. Darren staggered from the forest, crossed the lawn and stopped abruptly when he noticed his truck parked in the driveway. Maybe he was hallucinating, like when he saw the fawn. Maybe that was a hallucination too. He climbed onto the porch and pounded his fist against the front door. He pounded again, and eventually, the door creaked open. Brannon's body filled the doorway. He wore a red plaid shirt and blue jeans. Gray hair peppered his otherwise brown moustache. Darren now wished he'd tried to make it back to his own house instead of seeking help from Brannon, but when the heat from the wood fire wafted through the door, convulsive shivers shook his body.

Perhaps he'd momentarily blacked out, for he didn't know how he'd arrived to be standing in front of the wood stove wearing only his boxers. Alone at first, Darren was soon joined by Brannon's 16-year-old son, who entered the room without acknowledging him and sat on the couch to watch television. He had a gangly body with big hands and, Darren determined, a cynical smirk.

Darren felt the joints of his knees and hips loosen in the healing warmth. His fingers and toes burned with the sensation of blood flowing back into his extremities. Peggy appeared around the corner then, rushing to him as she held a heavy blue blanket that she draped over his shoulders. She hugged him, pressed her cheek against his chest, and felt about his face and neck asking if he was okay. Her touch felt outstanding. At first, he didn't know if he could speak, his teeth chattered so much. But he managed to say he was fine, and then wanted to know what she was doing here.

"I came looking for you. It was late. I was getting worried. Do you have any hot tea or anything like that?"

Brannon stood under the archway with his chubby arms folded across his thick chest. "Samuel, go get some hot water."

His son left the room without saying a word. Peggy asked Darren how he got wet.

"I fell in the pond," he said.

"My pond?" Brannon said.

"The ice gave way under me."

Peggy asked how he got out and Darren told her. "I lost my rifle," he said. "It slipped from my shoulder."

Samuel entered the room with a glass of water. He handed it to Darren and stood against the wall, nearer his father. "Somebody shot a doe on our property and left her to die," he said.

Darren drank the hot water, the heat at first burning his stomach. "She wasn't on your property when I shot her," he finally said.

"It was a shitty shot."

"Samuel," Brannon said.

Peggy asked if they could borrow some clothes to go home. Brannon left the room. Darren resisted the urge to ask Samuel if he'd seen the fawn nearby. Part of him hoped he'd hallucinated seeing the fawn. Brannon came back and set a pair of sweat pants, a tee shirt, and some cotton socks on the arm of a chair. "Keep 'em," he said.

As he dressed, Darren felt ridiculous, like a spectacle. Brannon and his son stood and stared, and Peggy didn't say anything. The sweat pants, tee shirt and socks were all too big. Darren had to bunch up the waistband of the sweat pants to keep them from slipping off his hips. He put his boots back on as Peggy gathered up his wet clothes. Dressed now, Darren said, "Who shot the doe?"

"I did," Brannon said.

Again, Darren wanted to ask about the fawn. Did he see her? Instead, he asked what he intended to do with the carcass.

"Coyotes got to eat, too. Besides, we got enough venison in the freezer to last us two years. Me and the boys have already filled our tags for the season."

Darren knew Brannon said this to piss him off — another way of saying Darren couldn't get his deer. Darren knew he had legal right to the deer, but he also knew that by morning the coyotes would have found the carcass and, perhaps, the fawn, too.

"One more thing," Brannon said, and Darren and Peggy stopped and stood in the doorway leading to the porch. "I told you before, no hunting on my property. Do it again and maybe next time I won't be so hospitable."

Darren wanted to curse Brannon but words escaped him. Peggy pulled on his arm, directing him down the steps and across the lawn to their truck.

Peggy drove home and asked Darren twice if he was okay. Darren, sitting silent, said he was fine, but he wasn't fine. He wasn't fine just like the night sky wasn't fine — a half moon silhouetting a few aimless clouds. There was no hope for the fawn. On a clear moonlit night such as this, the coyotes would track her easily.

After a steamy hot shower and a deep sound sleep, Darren was aroused early that next morning by Peggy's amorous caresses. He opened his eyes to find a corona of morning light about her luminous body: the most beautiful image he'd ever seen. She lowered herself onto him, and he discovered in the crook of her neck the scent of lavender.

They made love and then lay together without speaking. Part of Darren wanted to push Peggy away, demand to know why she went to Brannon's to look for him. Of all people. It was the humiliation he felt, and Peggy having witnessed it, that bothered him most — like the odd manner in which Brannon's boy Samuel refused to notice Darren even as he stood nearly naked in their living room.

Later that morning, Darren removed an old rifle from his gun cabinet, spread a towel over the kitchen table, disassembled the rifle, cleaned the components, and then reassembled it. "Haven't you had enough hunting for awhile?" Peggy said.

He removed three remaining apples from the wire basket on the counter and cut the apples into small slices. His idea, which he did not share with Peggy, was to attract the fawn with the apple slices, hopefully drawing her in close enough so that he could slip a rope around her neck and lead her home. A nature preserve, or even a zoo, might adopt the fawn, a better proposition, he thought, than the fawn managing a long winter on her own. "I hope you're not going onto Brannon's property again."

He tried to determine the significance of that question, but left without saying another word.

Darren stood along the rock wall that separated Brannon's property from the state land. The snow sparkled in the sunlight, the air dry and warm. Occasionally, clumps of snow crashed down from the treetops. He found the trail he'd taken the day before and followed it, figuring if he took the same trail Brannon wouldn't notice he'd crossed onto his property for a second time. He skirted the edge of the pond, noticing the watery hole he'd fallen into remained free of ice. On the opposite shore, he picked up the trail again and followed it until he discovered the doe's carcass — or what remained of it. Bloody paw prints trampled the snow. The disemboweled chest cavity and ribs remained, but the doe's head had been dragged off, as had her hindquarters.

Scouting the perimeter, Darren found no evidence of the fawn. If she'd stayed by her mother, which instinct would have properly dictated, then the coyotes had likely discovered her as well.

Darren followed the trail back to the state land and eventually returned to his own land, where he climbed into his tree stand and sat with the rifle across his lap. He felt remorse for the doe having suffered and more for the fawn left on her own, who had probably fallen prey to coyotes, yet a faint sense of jubilation also welled inside him for having escaped death, much like he had by being born. He balanced the dichotomy between these emotions with what he saw as nature's symbiosis: the roles of hunter and prey. There were those meant to survive and propagate — and those not.

Just over the knoll, Darren heard voices and laughing. The three Brannon boys, led by the oldest, Samuel, appeared walking beside the rock wall. Although they were close enough he could make out their expressions, he couldn't decipher what they were saying. Remembering Samuel's cynical smirk from the night before, Darren raised the rifle, aimed at the snow-covered branches above where the boys walked, and pulled the trigger. He missed. The reverberation of the rifle blast sucked out all other sound from the woods. The boys glanced frantically in all directions, never once sighting Darren in his tree stand. In fact, Samuel seemed to momentarily look right at him but not see Darren, quickly turning his attention in another direction. After a minute or two of quiet banter, the three boys turned and walked back down the knoll without a word.

A tremor passed through Darren's hands when he considered what he'd just done. Discharging a rifle in the direction of the three boys, even though he aimed high, was crazy. He felt disgusted and ashamed, more ashamed than the night he stood nearly naked in Brannon's living room. He climbed down from his tree stand and started home. His hunting season was over, that was for sure. He didn't feel like hunting anymore.

೧

Two days before Christmas, Darren left the county highway garage to begin what would amount to ten days off from work. Glancing into the rear-view mirror, the translucent reflection staring back at him no longer concerned or startled him. In fact, a strange feeling of anticipation filled him as he arrived home and entered the back door into the laundry room, where he kicked off his boots and hung his jacket in the closet. He called for Peggy, but she didn't answer.

Whistling, he walked down the hallway in his wool socks to discover her in the nursery tearing down the wallpaper she'd put up over a week ago. And the crib was gone.

"What are you doing?" Darren asked.

"I don't like this wallpaper," she said, her back to him as she tore a long strand of paper from the wall. "I changed my mind."

"Where's the crib?"

"I took it apart and stored it in the basement."

"Why?"

"Because we don't need it, and I want this room."

"For what?"

Peggy spun toward Darren, the wallpaper wrapping around her legs. "For something I want," she cried.

Peggy threw the wallpaper into a heap on the floor. Darren took a cautious step toward her. He knew the look on his wife's face. More intense than he'd ever seen before, but he knew this look. He knew what had happened. It had happened again, the same thing that happened every month.

SPECIAL SECTION: UCO@125

Old North Clock Tower with People in it

Number: A0031
Date: 1909 – 1921

Teresa Mirll

When first stepping onto the campus of the University of Central Oklahoma, visitors and incoming students will no doubt notice the towering structure of Old North, but many newcomers to UCO (as well as current students and faculty) may not know the historical significance of the clock tower. The first building on campus and the oldest higher education building in Oklahoma, Old North Tower underwent construction in the summer of 1892. Even before work was finished, excited teachers and students held the first classes in Old North, despite the lack of indoor heating, and only closed the school due to weather conditions when the inkwells froze.

The founders' passion for education, as well as for appreciating Old North, survives at UCO today. On November 9, 1972, exactly eighty-one years after a small group of students registered with The Normal School for the Territory of Oklahoma (now UCO), Old North was recognized as a national historic site. Since the closing of Old North in 2000 due to structural complications, UCO has received over $39 million in donations to renovate the building, including a $500,000 grant from the E.L. and Thelma Gaylord Foundation. President Don Betz expressed his gratitude to all who supported this project, proclaiming such generosity "a true testament to the important place Old North holds in not only our history, but the hearts of all Oklahomans." Continuing the tradition of honoring Old North, UCO now includes the Old North Walk as part of the commencement ceremony, as graduating students pass through the Gerald "Cowboy" Barnett Bell Plaza at Plunkett Park and touch the bell that hung overhead when the first twenty-seven students enrolled and that signalled the beginning of classes at the Territorial Normal School.

Bird's Eye View Of Edmond with Old North & Old South on Horizon

Number: EHF032
Date: 1915

Parker Hansen

"Oklahoma"

Powerful potential permeates,
For rain will come as Natives cry.
Bang! Clang! Societal sounds
Progress, never lies.

Romulan rainbows restore
A lost sense of self,
For on Second and Broad —
Past, present, and future fog.

Education, the constant, stands tall
Sustaining not one, but all,
Like water and bread,
Nourishment, then bed.

Students become teachers,
Teachers remain students.
Irony informs ideology,
Unyielding to insightful provocation

… and so we tread.
This dust has never been
So read.

People Gathering for Story Hour

Number: A0071
Date: 1915

Brandi Douglas-Clark

One-Hundred and Twenty-Five Years of Stories

"After nourishment, shelter and companionship, stories are the thing we need most in the world."
— Philip Pullman

Young women wear delicate blouses and high-waisted, ankle-length skirts trimmed with sashes and ribbon. Young men sit in three-piece lounge suits. Some have crowned their heads with broad hats, as they all gather on the grass to hear a story told. Maybe it's a short comedy, romance, or an adventure story. This is a genteel 1915 scene of young people coming together, on a lawn, while far away a Great War is raging. Little do they know that in just five short years the world, the country, and their lives will have been changed immeasurably.

Young woman wear tank tops, form-fitting leggings, or shorts. Young men wear ripped jeans and t-shirts. Some have crowned their heads with baseball caps or sunglasses, as they gather together, standing in the grass, to hear a story told. Maybe it's a short comedy, romance, or an adventure story, something they have read, learned, or experienced. You hear them speaking excitely to one another. This is a scene nearly one-hundred years later, while far away a war is raging. Little do they know what the next five years will bring or how the world, the country, and their own lives will change.

The importance of both scenes is not in the differences, but in the similarities. The stories: meant to inspire thought, imagination, conversation, and companionship. Here, on the grounds of this university, stories are told, taught, and created every day. No student leaves as the same person she or he was when he or she entered. They leave with new ideas and knowledge, all imparted by stories, new stories all their own that will help and guide their future selves in this ever changing world. One-hundred and twenty-five years of listening, learning, growing, and entertainment. If only the walls could talk. Imagine the stories they would tell.

Old North
in Winter Blanket of Snow

Number: A 1810
Date: 1913 – 1914

Mindy Teslewicz

The image of the winter blanket covering the campus in 1913-1914, although black and white, is a bold statement of the influence of an icon and the difference time can make. Old North, pictured not long after its birth, is covered in the purity of the snow. I believe that purity is still reflected today on the campus of the University of Central Oklahoma. Education stands to enlighten and change, not only the minds of the educated, but the lives of those touched by the educated.

In this scene, the background is sparse and seemingly flat. It appears desolate and ghostly. However, I believe that these qualities make this image the most hopeful. As a student at the modern-day UCO, I can see every change for the good. The campus is now crowded with people who are eager to learn and change the world. Our campus has indeed changed our part of the world. Today, we have added beautiful landscaping and have changed the landscape of education in Oklahoma.

The university has adapted in time to meet the needs of the community and Oklahoma's economy. Beginning as one of the first institutions of higher learning in our state, it is now the third-largest university in Oklahoma. UCO began as the Territorial Normal School of Oklahoma. As you can see from the photograph, it started from humble beginnings, with one building and a horse and carriage, and grew into a large suburban university that educates approximately 17,000 students! Our great campus may have started small, but all great things have to begin somewhere. I am pleased that our story began with Old North.

Students Hanging
"University" Sign After Name Change

Number: F0167
Date: 1970

Marianna Bennett

The name change depicted here was just one of many changes in the University of Central Oklahoma's long history. In fact, this name change was not even the first of the five that the campus went through before becoming most commonly known today as "UCO." Regardless of its name, UCO has always been known as the home of the bronze and blue, and as a community dedicated to education, leadership, and service. Since its foundation 125 years ago, UCO has been searching constantly for new ways to better itself as a university and as a community. One of the most beautiful things about UCO is how easily it welcomes these types of changes and improvements. From the first name change in 1904, to the new campus branch being built in downtown Oklahoma City during 2014, our campus has been growing and creating an even bigger community, and the students, staff, and faculty continue to be excited and supportive. The students are driven to elicit changes, too, bettering the campus for each subsequent generation and passing on their abundant enthusiasm. The school spirit and sense of community here at UCO hard to rival, and its dedication to transformation is stronger than ever. The Latin inscription on UCO's coat of arms perfectly sums up this passion for change in just a few words: *Ubi Motus Est,* "Where the Movement Is."

English Teacher at Desk in Old South

Number: A0044
Date: 1909 – 1921

Christina Morel

Through just a single glance, it is difficult not to notice the thoughtful, welcoming, and pleasant gaze of this young woman and to take heed of the carefully aligned papers and books on her desk. Her stance exhibits leadership, and her surroundings encompass the spirit, hard work, and determination of a student at the University of Central Oklahoma. Her mind, like the outstretched plants around her, has been transformed through her schooling. Her chosen topic of study, English, displays her devotion to the written word –- a subject that thrives on research, imagination, history, and the beauty of human thought and language. Each student has a passion she or he pursues in our classrooms, and our university leads our students in the right direction.

As we reach our 125th anniversary, we are reminded of how much we have grown as a university. This photograph captures the opportunity and stability that our campus offers its students. Our welcoming students and staff, whom we see daily working hard at their desks to create a brighter future, are the individuals who mold our campus community into the memorable and diverse place it is today. You can look at any of our students and see the same memorable gaze and stance as this young woman displays. Our institution will continue to thrive for many years to come, because the students who sit at our desks exhibit the wealth of knowledge our university holds dear.

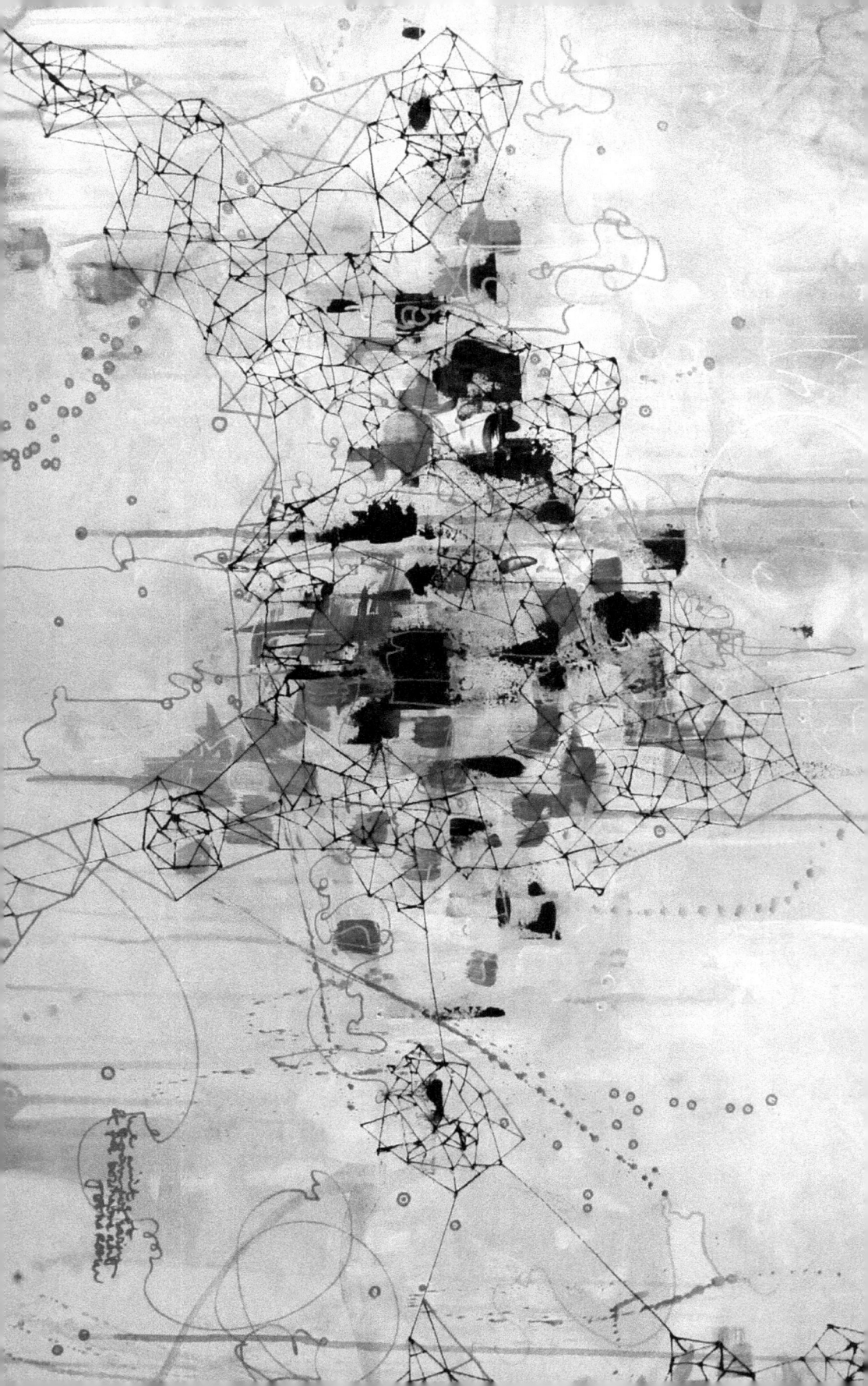

NON-FICTION

Colored Memories

Terry Barr

Somewhere in the autumn of first grade, Mrs. Baird hands out an outlined page for us to color. It's a scene in a neighborhood much like ours. A tree-lined block, and as you gaze down that sidewalk, you notice a little girl coming your way. She's holding her schoolbooks flat against her chest, as girls do. You can't quite see the details of her face, but in my mind, she's smiling. Her long hair hangs behind her in a ponytail. Leaves are falling to the ground, and in the distance, a school bus heads away from the school and away from our girl, leaving her alone and ripe for the taking. Her parents must trust her. They must have read all the safety rules to her. And they must think nothing bad could possibly happen in their quaint little community.

I often walked home too, but never alone — at least not until third grade when I knew better how to stay on the straightest path; the direct route up 19th street, five blocks to home. On the milder first grade afternoons, five of us would walk home together: Mary Jane, Laurie, Randy, Ted and me. It was the fall of 1962, and it seems impossible now to think back to that time and consider all that was about to happen in Alabama, in the South. In our nation.

But back to our coloring scene. As the girl gets closer, we can see, though she can't, someone else watching her. A man on the left lurking behind an enormous oak tree. You might call him a harbinger of all that will befall us in the coming years. He's a white man. His uncolored face has the blackest eyes I've ever seen. Does he even have eyeballs, and if so, how do I color them? He's hiding but ready for his chance, which is approaching as surely as all the days and weeks of our coming holiday season. As hidden as he is for this moment, he's hiding something even deeper behind his back.

A bag with the word "Candy" written on it.

Mrs. Baird explains to us that the picture is trying to teach us something:

"Never accept candy from a stranger and never go with someone you don't know, even if they seem nice and say they know you. This little girl doesn't know this man. Do you think she'll take his candy? Would you?"

When Mrs. Baird finishes, we begin our coloring. Blue skies, red and gold leaves, green or brown grass depending on how observant we are of our fathers' yard work. But when it gets to the bag of candy, our views diverge sharply. Some color it blue-violet, others brick red, and still others completely black.

Brenda Sue Stokes, however, pulls the yellow-orange Crayola from her pack of sixty-four. When we finish, it is her bag that stands out amongst all the others, a phosphorescence that eventually wins her first prize in the Responsible Citizen Coloring Contest. Her drawing will hang on the wall outside the principal's office the rest of the year.

The funny thing is though I never would accept candy from a stranger because of the color she used, because of the perfect way she kept that color within those candy bag lines leaving the word as clear and prominent as before, I want that bag of candy. I want to grab it and open it and eat everything inside. It even scares me a little bit how badly I want that bag.

In those years, I don't think I knew or heard of any kid getting taken by a stranger, and even if there was, I wonder *if* our parents would have told us, or *what* they would have told us. For what can you tell a six-year old about abuse, torture, and rape? About vulnerability and things that can happen if you aren't cautious and careful?

About what can happen when you walk home alone.

Or when you ride a bicycle against cautioning lights, bells, or whistles.

I I

It's true that kids don't always listen to their teacher's lessons. Thinking back on it now, I don't know why our teachers didn't ask us to color a new picture every day given how many dangers and predators and things there are that go screaming through the night or mid-afternoon.

We could have colored a beach scene with gulls flying overhead. After a picnic lunch, little Mary might want to jump back into the ocean, but her pretty mommy asks her politely to sit by her and make a sand castle for an hour or so until her food digests.

Or a scene of a pleasant neighborhood with storm clouds hovering, and a particular funnel-looking cloud about to descend on a boy and his mom as they try to take groceries out of the trunk of their station wagon.

Or a scene of a city street with a friendly policeman on the corner blowing his whistle to prevent Susie and Freddy from crossing against the light.

Or maybe this scene:

A double train track running right through the center of town. Its guardrails are descending, the red lights flashing, and four blocks away to the left, the engine of the Southern Railroad line bears down, horn blaring for all it's worth. It's heading to Nashville, maybe carrying coal or warehouse goods or new building materials. It has certainly slowed a bit, but since it's not stopping in this little town, it's still moving at 40-50 mph. Of course everyone else stops: the cars, the pedestrians, even old crazy Joe with his steering wheel. We'll never know, however, why one boy on a bicycle doesn't — why he tries to beat that train. Is he running late on his newspaper delivery route? Is he showing off? Does he enjoy living dangerously? Or does he sincerely believe he can glide between the wooden guardrails and slip past the moving hunk of iron and metal?

This would have been a coloring lesson to consider. Who knows whether any of us would have heeded it, or remembered it a few years later when it should have mattered to this nine-year-old boy? Surely, you say, we got the message about waiting for trains from our parents, teachers, society at large, and I suppose we did. I know I did, though I have to confess that even now in my late fifties, when I hear the train-horn or see the guardrails lowering, I wonder if I can beat it. And if I believe I can, I do.

But on April 8, 1967, I was ten, and Terry Blaine Wenndt was only nine. One grade ahead of him, I knew him only as another fourth grader, another face in the hallway, another body running over the playground.

Another ghostly presence in the world of pre-adolescence.

I remember him vividly only through the photograph I saw in the paper the week after the accident. A photo of a butch-cut blond, smiling boy who looked as normal as he could be. What wasn't normal, though, was the way he'll always be remembered: as a headless torso, bloodied and mangled and dead for no reason.

I heard all sorts of things after the fact: his head was completely severed; his legs too. His torso was dragged for three city blocks. The engineer saw him but couldn't stop that speeding train. Much later, I'll hear that he tried to beat the train, that his front tire got caught in the rail groove, that he didn't want to leave his bike behind. How can anyone know these things? What evidence remains? What else can we do but wonder and talk about it?

April 8, 1967. In the days before the accident, we were listening as the double-sided hit "Penny Lane/Strawberry Fields Forever" released itself "there beneath [our] blue suburban skies." Such a happy tune. Just over a year to the day later, we are mourning or in some cases celebrating (for this *is* Alabama) when Dr. King is assassinated in Memphis on a cold and cloudy day.

What is the matter with April?

It ushers in the timeless season of baseball, yet it's also the "cruelest month." It brings the "showers" so necessary for "May flowers." It contains both Hitler's birthday and Holocaust Remembrance Day. And Tax Day. It began the Civil War and ended Lincoln's life. It finds itself at the very beginning of Chaucer's semi-fictional pilgrimage, usually at the ending of "Our Lord's" time on earth, and fully incorporating the Angel of Death's passing over the houses of the enslaved Israelites.

In 2011, April 27th brought a series of deadly tornados through Tuscaloosa, Alabama, and near my mother's house in Bessemer. I was with her on that day. It felt like a day at the beach at first: balmy and increasingly windy. Unwisely, we stayed in the area instead of driving north and far away to complete safety. A day earlier, I had visited the scene of a similar tornado that passed through several years before. The 2011 tornado traveled that very same path, mercifully sparing our house. These events, of course, are entirely natural.

April 2014. More tornados, veering slightly northeast of their familiar path. Again, my mother's house isn't damaged, though a piece of aluminum the size of a Toyota Corolla lodges itself in a front oak tree. Two blocks away, both houses and trees are uprooted. The path diagonally dissects the older part of town. I have no information on deaths or injuries, but I know that the tornado's path leads it right over the spot where Terry Wenndt tried to cross a double train track forty-seven years earlier to the month.

April 7, 1967, my father celebrates his forty-first birthday. My mother makes his favorite banana pudding in lieu of cake. We are all carefree and happy. As maybe the Wenndt family was on this night. The night before their lives were so unnaturally torn.

III

When I begin my research, I don't know the right year of the accident. I contact the Birmingham Public Library, but they see no record of such an accident in 1962, the year I think it must have happened. I contact the Bessemer Library by email, but they never reply to my query. I tell my frustrations to my brother Mike, and it's he who first alerts me that my memory isn't as precise as I think:

> "The boy's name was Terry Wenndt, and he had an older brother named Randy. I was in the car with Mom, and we had to drive near the scene. I remember seeing a lot of cars, and the train stopped somewhere between 18th and 19th streets. We knew something bad had happened."
>
> "I must not have been with you," I say, for surely I would have remembered. "Did y'all stop?"
>
> "No, Momma didn't want to. But I think I was in the first grade with his younger brother Timmy." Which would have made me a fifth grader.
>
> Mike's memory is like those ice skating blades spewing shards of rink when the Olympian lands after a triple axle. I have no doubt he's right.
>
> Next, I call my childhood friend Joe.
>
> "You probably won't know what I'm talking about, but do you remember a little boy being killed by a train when we were growing up?"
>
> "I remember exactly!" He's almost yelling. "I was there! My brother Jon, Pam Cowley, and I were riding our bikes, and we had just stopped to talk to this guy. I don't remember his name, and we didn't know him well. We were just kids on bikes riding downtown.

After we rode away, I heard the train coming. Then the screech, and then an awful sound. We turned around and rode back. There was blood e-v-e-r-y-w-h-e-r-e. And body parts. I must have been eleven or twelve, and it scared me. It changed me."

Is it wrong that his memory excites me? That I feel like I did when I uncovered forty boxes of old comic books at a junk store in Missoula, Montana once? That I have another in my series of "strange Bessemer deaths" to write about?

I begin obsessing about this story. I can't get back to Bessemer for another few weeks, but it hits me that someone has set up a "Fond Memories of Bessemer" page on Facebook. On November 12 at 11:20 am, I post a question about the death of Terry Wenndt. The first response comes in eleven minutes later. For the next three days, my phone app lights up regularly, chillingly, thrillingly. I learn so much about the accident, about old Bessemer friends, and people I might never have thought of again.

It's like coloring a blank page.

IV

I wonder if it's his name or the circumstances that stir so many people's memories of Terry Wenndt. One person remembers that her first grade class all walked together to the church for his funeral. Another person says her mother went to comfort Terry's mother, bringing food and warmth as people normally do in times of death.

What Cindey Huckabee remembers are the nightmares that followed her for weeks after seeing his casket.

A girl I knew back then, Allison McDonald Arnett, writes that when she saw my post, she quickly contacted her sister Lynn who told Allison that Terry "...was in her class the year it happened:

> "We were in the grocery store [the A&P on Carolina Avenue], just across the street from the train tracks, with our mother when the train hit Terry. That's why it's so ingrained in my memory," Allison says. "I always thought, and Lynn confirmed, that he tried to beat the train, and his bike either got stuck on the tracks or he fell while crossing. Lynn thinks her teacher was in the store, too, when it happened. She also remembers going home and watching the news that evening, and that's when she learned who was in the accident."

Another old friend, Don Bowen, says that his father, a special agent in charge of investigating "wrecks, accidents, and thefts" for Southern Railroad, "worked the accident."

And Susie Seals, who was in my first grade class and with me off and on throughout high school, googled the accident. The date, she says, was

Saturday, April 8, 1967.

So finally I can place time. I can confirm my brother's memory. I was in the fifth grade during that spring, Mrs. Shivers' class. Allison's sister Lynn was a grade behind me, making both she and Terry Wenndt fourth graders, in either Miss Ball's or Mrs. Harwell's class.

At the tail end of the Fond Memories of Bessemer responses came one from another boy I knew back then, Yogi Padalino:

"I live in the house that Terry lived in back then. His brother stopped by a while back. He has two brothers — Randy and Timmy. The address is 1508 Dartmouth Avenue."

Five blocks from my family's house, but we didn't know them at all. So close, and yet, so far.

V

Memories fade, but return violently when enough people contribute to the remembering.

Thanksgiving weekend 1967, outside that same A&P on Carolina Avenue, just a few hundred yards from where Terry Wenndt was crushed on those train tracks, the janitor of our church is shot in the heart by a distraught white man whose wife left him that afternoon.

A month later, Christmas time, I receive my first ever bicycle, a red Skyrider. My parents forbid me to ride it in the street, however, which leaves me coasting down the sidewalk. The following summer, they relent, and I am free to travel anywhere, even over railroad tracks. I don't understand why they worry so much. I know the streets are dangerous, but all my friends ride them. I never come close to having an accident, and as I ride, it's like that boy and the train never collided, never even met. He fades away, and it's as likely as not then that he'll fade away for good. Forever.

And yet, here he is before me. What is the trigger? Is it that my thoughts have turned to death in my hometown? Or that I'm overseeing my college students drawing and coloring their own graphic novels, the memories of their lives? Or that I'm asking my creative nonfiction students to investigate a scene from their past and that their accounts are so deep and personal that I can't stand the beauty and the often horrifying tragedy?

Or is it that recently my wife and I have taken to biking on the Swamp Rabbit Trail in our current home in Greenville, SC, she on her brand new Schwinn 20-speed, I on my K-Mart tourist bike, as similar to the one I had in 5th grade as I can get? Red, with no gears.

At one point on the trail we have to negotiate train tracks. There's a sign posted nearby asking you to be cautious, or perhaps even to walk your bike across. In any case, you're supposed to cross the tracks perpendicularly to keep your tires from getting stuck. Once, we waited for ten minutes as a slow train approached. I'll admit that at first, when I saw it coming, I was tempted to urge us to go faster, to race ahead and beat it. But there were others in front of us, adults and a few little boys and girls. We weren't in any hurry, had no place we'd rather be. So the saner part of me relaxed into the waiting, believing that time would pass as it's supposed to. That soon enough the other side would appear, and we'd be on our way to the end of the trail and the Leopard Forest Coffee Company. Wholly and happily.

It's a belief I would have liked Terry Wenndt to imagine.

And draw.

A picturesque scene he could have colored of all the days he should have had.

Off the Record

Morgan Sorrell

I look out the helicopter and see enemy troops miles farther along than our intel said they'd be, so they're just right fucking *there*. They fire, and even though there's wind everywhere, I can smell smoke coming from somewhere...

I look out the helicopter again, and now it's on fire. I can hear the alarms going off in the pilot's helmet because that's how goddamn many there are. He reaches up and pulls a lever, and I smell the stuff that's supposed to put the fire out — some sort of powder shit. But it's not enough because there are too many bullet holes, too much fire, wind everywhere.

And the ground keeps getting closer. I grab the gun and sweep it sideways in an arc, then I'm half rolling and half stumbling away from the crash. I brace myself for enemy fire, but there's no one left to shoot. I got them all before we even hit the ground.

"Is everybody OK?!" the pilot shouts.

I try to speak into the mic in my helmet, but for some reason, I can't force out any words. It's hard enough just to breathe. I don't feel so well. I lean back and see my buddy. He's got a hole in his head, and his brains are against the side of the helicopter.

The next time I open my eyes, I'm in a new helicopter — one that I pray isn't on fire — and it's a medic who's screaming, "Are you OK?!"

I don't know. You're the medic. You tell me.

Later, I find out that I was shot three times, in a diagonal line across my chest, from shoulder to hip. Thank God for vests, but it hurt like a sonofabitch. The first shot dislocated my shoulder, and the second two broke my ribs. Not that I ever got a purple heart for any of that. The mission wasn't "on the record," and you can't get medals for missions that "didn't happen."

I wonder if that means my buddy "didn't die."

Sleeping Under the Stars

Matt Berman

It was our first day back in Yellowstone National Park — late April — and Nathan and I were already on the first hike of the summer season. He was walking ahead of me on the Beaver Ponds Trail, just starting to turn a corner around a few small trees, when suddenly he stopped. I'd been concentrating on my boots breaking through the thin plates of ice that had filled the trail, and so I nearly crashed into him. He was standing there like a statue. By the serious look on his face, I could tell he was trying to hear something.

"You don't think," I started to say. But Nathan just held up his index finger and kept staring, cutting me off mid-sentence. *That's our Bear* is what I wanted to say. After all, the trail we'd been hiking had been closed for a week or so, ever since a mother grizzly bear bluff-charged a park employee there. We'd decided to hike it anyway just to see what would happen.

Nathan already knew what I was thinking. We made eye contact and he nodded. He'd read my mind. This was our bear. Then he heard those same low grunts again; I could see the fear in his eyes. But I still hadn't heard the noise that'd frozen Nathan in place.

But then I heard it too, a low guttural sound emanating from the otherwise quiet forest, a single gruff note repeated three times, so low we almost couldn't hear it. *Whua, Whua, Whua.*

Grinning with fright, so that I could see his teeth and the whites of his eyes, Nathan pointed to the left of the trail, at a cluster of trees that seemed to be where our bear was holed up. Twice more we heard the growls, three at a time, with a moment of absolute silence in between.

Then, suddenly, a sapling tree started swaying violently back and forth. Instantly I was backpedaling, watching as Nathan did the same, and I was looking beyond him at the tree until we rounded the corner and it disappeared out of sight.

We watched that bend in the trail just long enough to make sure a bear hadn't stepped out in our direction, wasn't about to charge us. When we felt sure it wasn't, and we felt safe enough to turn our backs, we did, and we went straight back to the trailhead where we'd started.

Back within sight of our village, we let our guards down enough to laugh. Nothing was funny, but our reflexive chuckle released the stress of our first encounter with a grizzly. We were lucky Nathan had been so perceptive, instinctively freezing us in place like prey animals trying to avoid detection. And we were lucky that bear decided to let us off with a warning.

"We probably should have known better," I said to Nathan, but he just shrugged his shoulders and said, "Eh," as if to say: *we survived, though, right?* That hike set the tone for the summer — two unprepared, rule-breaking, ignorant East Coast kids, the product of a modern age, sent back through time, into the Yellowstone Backcountry, only to be predictably humbled. Whether grizzly bear, an unforgiving act of Mother Nature, or some misjudgment on our part, something always sent us running away from the primitive world just as fast as we'd been trying to escape into it.

‿

The month before that I'd had my epiphany, as Nathan and I backpacked through Canyonlands National Park and the Vermillion Cliffs Wilderness. That brief glimpse into the world of backpacking opened my eyes to a whole new path. At twenty-three years old, I was suddenly obsessed with sleeping outdoors. When we moved back to Mammoth Hot Springs to start the summer, I started sleeping outside every night.

Now I couldn't stand to be in buildings — the dorm where I lived, the restaurant where I worked, any of them. Of course I'd spent the majority of my life in buildings (most of us do), those artificial ecosystems with their floors covered in carpet and water fountains bubbling with drinking water and artificial lights shining down from above, like imitation grass, waterfalls, sunshine. In our efforts to shut nature out we can't help but mimic it.

Even most of the people I worked with in Yellowstone lived their days almost completely within a tangled network of buildings — dorms, shops, cafeteria, restaurant — and at night back to the dorms and to the bar. And I'm not against bars. But there in Yellowstone, all I could think about from inside those buildings was how the walls were blocking our view of the national park all around us, and how the ceilings were blocking our view of the sky.

In small doses, breaks from their usual lives, most everyone there went on a least the occasional hike, which sent them walking through the unaltered world as humans had always known it, before we so drastically changed our environment to our liking. But now, unfamiliar, we walk the wild earth tepidly, scared of what might happen. Even of Yellowstone's millions of yearly visitors, only three percent, on average, leave the pavement and boardwalks, and step onto the dirt trail, which is where you really start to enter the forest. I guess we've always been scared to be away from the village. And that's why we built our buildings in the first place. In the early days, just as today, maybe only the most adventurous fools would've left their communities on extended quests into the unknown.

‿

Even though the mountains were just starting to lose their snow, I was desperate to sleep out under the stars. So I climbed a metal ladder to get onto the roof of the Dorm.

Sleeping on the roof gave me an unparalleled view of the sky, but I was still laughably on the line between civilization and the wild country surrounding it. Everything about that environment except for the crisp night air and the stars was something that would have been truly foreign — frightening even — to our long-ago ancestors. I was still resting my head against unnatural things like whatever weird rubber covered the steel and concrete skeleton of that roof. And I could still hear the puffing of the vents, and see the lights from the building. But if I just kept looking up and breathing, I could block all that out.

Lying there on my back, looking up at the stars, I finally felt at home. I took a deep breath, pulling cold air deep into my lungs. In the silence of solitude, I could finally think. Is the oxygen concentration higher out in the open air than in a stuffy dorm room? And is the carbon dioxide concentration higher indoors? Don't three or four people (or eight) in a closed-up dorm room, watching a movie, eventually use up a significant portion of their oxygen? Don't they gradually fill the air with carbon dioxide? Is the difference enough for me to notice? There had to be a physical reason it felt so good to be outside.

Nothing obstructed the stars from that rooftop. No trees blocked the view, no clouds, no light or air pollution, no humidity. On cold nights like that one, a small window in the sleeping bag exposed just enough of my face to allow me to breathe and to see the stars, hundreds for every one I'd ever seen from the East Coast. I'd never known how bright the night sky could be.

Thinking about the incomprehensible distances the light from those stars had just traveled, ending, after thousands of light years, on my eyeball, gave me energy. I was excited about the adventures in store for the summer. As I faded out to sleep, compulsively thinking about getting up into the mountains, honing my backpacking skills, seeing first hand what the Yellowstone backcountry had to offer, I watched shooting stars streak across the sky one after another until I could no longer keep my eyelids open.

⟲

But that society I was halfway trying to flee had me by a short tether. Working in the restaurant kept me in the civilized world, gave me a place to park my car, a way to make enough money to survive, and a central location to begin my forages into the wild. It gave me a place to come back to, or, more realistically, a place to be pulled away from.

The next night, I wandered up a small drainage where the village ended and the forest began, quickly finding an old, gnarled evergreen tree with a flat spot underneath it just big enough to lie down in, a good place to set up a semi-permanent camp. That little hideout gave me a commanding view of the community of Mammoth Hot Springs, with its cluster of civilization — red-roofed colonial buildings, ringed with roads and trails and telephone lines, the night air filled with hazy electric light and reeking subtly of car exhaust. And I could see out across the primitive land east of the village, the foothills and canyons. Nestled into that spot, I was completely out of the way, far from any road or hiking trail, and almost impossible to see from down below.

I propped up a few Y-shaped limbs against the tree's trunk, creating a skeleton that I could stretch my tarp across if it rained. But that night was clear, so I just slept out with nothing but my sleeping bag and a thin foam pad.

At that critical point in time when the Internet took control of the world and rural people around the world were moving to urban areas en masse, I wasn't moving to the city and diving into technology. That was just about the time that cell phones become completely ubiquitous. After I told my mother I'd been sleeping outside, she made me get one — but I could only pick up a signal from a few choice spots in the park, mostly in the villages, rarely out on the trail. I was doing exactly the opposite of what most people were doing. I was learning to survive in the primitive world.

The Gallatin Range, west of Mammoth, accessed only by thin hiking trails, was still the vast expanse of pristine forest and meadow and mountain that it had been since the glaciers last retreated. An impressive list of predators lived back there: black bears, grizzly bears, mountain lions, wolverines, wolves.

On that night, as I sat there contemplating the wildlife all around me, I was sure that I was one of the only humans on the wilderness side of the line, even though I could still see the village. And I still felt more comfortable sleeping outside than in the dorm.

But my comfort partly came from ignorance. In that first month of the summer, I was still doing most things wrong. Just two months earlier Nathan and I dove headfirst into backpacking. Though we'd known nothing about the high desert, we somehow survived that first five-day trip through Canyonlands, with more help from luck than skill. Now we began to explore Yellowstone with the same audacity. Looking back, we were just as unprepared in Yellowstone as we had been in the desert.

The first morning at my new spot was so silent I could hear an elk grinding its teeth as it nibbled at baby shoots of grass just a few feet away. The air smelled alive with Spring, and the valley was completely melted out, but I could still see feet of snow blanketing the surrounding mountains. What would it have been like to live before the rise of agriculture and industry? Or before cities and highways, before we so thoroughly constructed our own set of indoor environments? Before our population exploded? If I thought about it long enough, I could put myself in the mind frame of our ancient ancestors. I liked being there.

In the spring, each day was longer than the last, as the sun grew higher overhead, awakening a cold world from the prolonged, high-altitude winter. In the life of an earth worshiper, that increase in sunshine was reason to celebrate.

To me, it was the start of a new year. My resolution was to walk all the trails that snaked through the Yellowstone backcountry. At the time, I didn't feel like socializing with the people from all around the country I worked with down in the village. It's too bad I didn't spend more time with them. I could have learned something. But my attraction to life out in the forest overwhelmed any desire I had to get to know people. Plus in the previous year, I'd discovered that seasonal life makes it difficult to form lasting friendships.

I'd spent the previous summer in Oregon, and left behind a set of new friends there, and then a short season in Yellowstone, after which I also parted ways with amazing people, most of whom I haven't ever seen since. Then, after two months traveling the desert, I started another season in Yellowstone. But I knew I'd only be in Mammoth for a month before I moved again, to Canyon, another small village in the center of the park, for the rest of the summer. And I already knew that summer gig would only last three months. My life was in constant flux. I had no reason to devote energy to setting down roots.

My first shelters came out awful. It all seemed so simple in my head, *just tie the string to a few trees, throw the tarp over it, and tie down the ends.* But in the beginning it almost never worked like I'd planned it. Those first shelters left me exposed to whatever weather we'd set out into. Which meant snow and more snow on the way to Fawn Pass. On our second attempt, I'd somehow accidentally oriented my tarp's highest end straight into the prevailing winds. That night gusting winds brought in thick snow squalls, and I woke up covered in snow

But we weren't starting with a cleared-out campground, either, which would've helped me build a beginner's structure. Nathan and I were stubborn (maybe arrogant is better) in the way that early-twenties males often are. So we didn't get backcountry permits for those first trips. Instead, we "coyoted out" meaning we camped away from the trail, and used lightweight shelters, instead of merely assembling prefabricated tents in developed campgrounds. That strategy, we found out, worked much better on dry ground than on snow and ice.

Our distaste for tents was less about our affinity for ultralight backpacking (back then I hadn't even heard of it) than it was a rejection of doing things like everyone else did. Anyway, making shelters with tarp and string seemed more like a genuine adventure than setting up premade tents over flat ground.

And so a pattern began to emerge. Each excursion into the woods ended with us decidedly humbled by wild beast or Mother Nature, as we had been by the grizzly bear on the Beaver Ponds Trail, and as we were weeks later, by the feet of snowpack that still covered the ground and by the June snow squalls. Our first two attempts at the Gallatins were cut short, but that experience improved our shelter-building skills and cemented our resolve. Waking up wet was inspiration to improve.

By the end of June, when we walked out to Mount Holmes, we knew our survival skills were improving. We'd traveled seven miles through the backcountry to get there, crossing over the outlet of Grizzly Lake on a sea of floating timber, to a horse camp at the base of the mountain.

The wind and rain battered us for the entire first day of our trip, straight through the night and into the next morning. But between the two of us we had four tarps, which we tied together into a mega structure that afforded us the luxury of lounging about comfortably, drinking whiskey as we dried our wet clothes by the campfire. That daylong rainstorm climaxed with ground-shuddering thunder and gale-force winds, but we stayed dry and happy throughout.

The next day, when the sun finally came out, we left camp to walk to the top of the peak. By the time we arrived at the summit, we'd been hiking uphill for an hour and a half. We'd tromped over the snowpack for the final thousand feet, and the slush had thoroughly soaked my cotton shoes, which were never meant to be on top of Mount Holmes. *I need to start wearing boots,* I was thinking, instead of the Reebok Classics I'd been hiking in up to that point.

Nathan and I sat down on the steps of the old, boarded-up lookout cabin. At that moment, a small animal came rushing out of the woodpile, bounded a few paces, turned, stopped, and stared us down. It was so close I could see that it had long claws and a mouth overflowing with teeth.

The image of that strange creature staring at us contemptuously is still ingrained in my memory. I can see that predator's tank-like figure, small but stocky, its unruly skunk-like haircut, those teeth.

I stood up and yelled, *"A fisher cat!"* I threw my fists into the air. As animals are quick to do in the wild, it disappeared into the stunted mountain top forest in a few brief athletic moves. Maybe my misidentification had offended it.

We were left to catch our breath. And exchange high fives. Later I learned that what we'd confronted on the summit of Mount Holmes wasn't a fisher cat. It was one of the most rarely seen animals in the forest: a wolverine. Fierce fighters and extreme recluses, wolverines are known to have territories covering hundreds of square miles. It's estimated that only something like thirty to fifty wolverines are spread out across all of the Rocky Mountains south of Glacier National Park. They're the embodiment of freedom, independence, self-reliance, survival, wilderness.

~⊝~

After that trip, I had the satisfaction of knowing I'd been somewhere. Traversing great swaths of untamed land on foot made me feel alive like nothing else ever had. This was the environment in which humans had evolved. It all felt familiar to my instincts. It was where I was supposed to be. My awakening to the psychedelic feeling of living outside in our National Parks was like suddenly gaining a new tactile sense. The weather, the animals, the sun were the factors that directly affected my days. I'd become a worshiper of the literal sun, a born again caveman. One thing is for sure: I'd fully started to move in the opposite direction of everybody else around me.

And I'd been set free. I guess by exploring a place until my feet and back were contentedly tired was just my way of getting over the nervous energy of my youth, or my reaction to the pent-up feeling of growing up on the East Coast. In Yellowstone, I'd found the opposite of the East Coast.

~⊝~

With each passing weekend, Nathan and I were gaining more confidence. We'd learned to abandon our cotton clothes, which can stay cold for a long time if they get wet and pull away most of a person's hard-earned heat. And water was all around us in Yellowstone; it came from the sky as rain, snow, mist and fog; from the ground as dew and frost; collected here and there as lakes, rivers, streams and waterfalls; it came from us, as sweat that soaked through our shirts and socks.

By July, we'd learned to bring enough food. We'd also learned how to make more efficient meals (no more ramen noodles or white bread sandwiches). We rediscovered butter. And started making greasy pancakes for breakfast instead of instant oatmeal. More efficient foods meant we could stay out longer, and the longer we stayed out, the more alive we felt.

Nathan was almost as crazy about getting outside as I was. That's part of the reason we got along so well. Sleeping in the dorm room didn't bother him, like it bothered me, though, mostly because I was his roommate. Since I preferred to sleep outdoors, that left him with a private room, a commodity in the dorms. We were both happy with the arrangement.

My childhood obsession with a book called *My Side of the Mountain* could be one reason I found myself revolting against the modern world in my twenties. But who's to say? Did my repeated reading of that book plant a seed in my subconscious, which would cause me to run away to the woods years later? Or did I only love that book exactly because I was wired to be attracted to the wilderness from the beginning? Or maybe I'd just watched too many nature documentaries over the years.

It was early August before we finally made it to Fawn Pass, high up in the Gallatins, the place we'd been on our way to in June, when we'd built those faulty shelters and suffered through snowy nights. The errors of those harsh trips helped us learn what we needed to do better to survive. Now summer was finally breaking through. Wildflowers grew through thick grass. Ironically, now that we knew how to build shelters, we no longer needed them.

What we found far away on Fawn Pass, at the headwaters of the Gardiner River after such a long wait was Grizzly Bear Heaven. No official park service signs warned us about grizzly bears like they had on the Beaver Ponds Trail back in April. The signs of grizzly bears, however, were everywhere: huge piles of bear shit and giant tracks in the mud, with far-reaching claw marks. The only defense we had was telepathic communication. *We mean no harm. And we don't taste good, either.*

That next morning, I was struggling to start the campfire when I looked up just in time to see a young grizzly bear slowly lumbering into our backcountry camp; it stopped in a shaft of sunlight and extended its face upward, sniffing the air.

Across from that bear, not far away at all, I watched Nathan stand up out of his tent, shirtless and squinting into the sun, stretching his arms to the sky.

Nathan and the young grizzly bear, equally groggy and potentially thinking about breakfast, started wandering toward each other, both unaware of the other's presence.

When I yelled "*HEY!*" both Nathan and the bear looked up into each other's eyes. They watched each other, both of them deeply startled, for what felt like a really long second. Finally, the bear made its decision. In a moment, it turned and darted away.

Nathan exhaled, shook his head a few times. What else can a guy do? That same day, as we hiked, we startled two more bears, coming face to face with each one for a terrified second or so. Each encounter nearly stopped my heart. But without fail, the bear chose flight over fight. I don't know why. Maybe telepathy really works on bears.

With our heavy backpacks straining against our shoulders, we covered hundreds of miles of trail that summer, walking anywhere between thirty and fifty miles each weekend. Every trip revealed at least a small spark of Yellowstone's magic. But toward the end of the summer came a dramatic change — Nathan and I started to travel separately. Our work schedules didn't match up perfectly anymore, and so we started venturing out on those same wide-ranging trips, but now each of us walked solo journeys.

In those long afternoons (especially if the sky happened to be overcast), I couldn't help but to give in to my internal monologue. That was the first time I'd been completely immersed in solitude. Emotionally, living alone has a palpable effect on the soul. I started over thinking every last detail of my life. It only took a few hours before I took on a distant stare. But now I felt even more like Sam Gribley in *My Side of the Mountain*, making a life for myself in the woods.

Unconsciously, I'd stopped talking out loud; there was no reason to. In that state, I could go days without speaking. I wonder how many people have gone their entire lives without spending a single day in silence. In that silence, I contemplated my life. At the peak of the season, I could see the end just a few months away, and I had no idea what I was going to do, or where I was going to go.

In August, as I climbed west along the spine of the Sky Rim toward Bighorn Peak, I was in a trance-like state. The sun was already high up in the sapphire sky. Walking on that ridge I could see forever, north through Paradise Valley and south all the way across Yellowstone, to the Grand Tetons beyond that.

On that trip, Nathan and I had set out from opposite sides of a forty-mile trail, me from just south of Mammoth, and Nathan from twenty miles north of the town of West Yellowstone. So we were on the same path, walking mirror-image trips, opposite but the same. I passed the first two days, walking west, up and over two mountain passes; Electric and Sportsman, silently. At that point, Nathan and I camped together for a night though Nathan didn't show up until after sunset. And we really only spoke a few words to each other that night. It wasn't that there was any animosity between us; we'd just adapted to living quietly, both absorbed into our journeys.

The next morning when we parted ways, headed in opposite directions, Nathan was excited for me to walk the section of trail he'd just walked, which climbs to the Sky Rim and the high lakes of the Gallatin Range. "Really cool up there," he said before he left. "Seems like great mountain lion country."

A full day later, I was once again completely entranced with the sight of my boot tops pounding away the miles underneath me, feeling as if somehow under their own power. I'd gotten out of camp early that day, easy to do on a solo trip. If there's no one to talk to, there's really no reason to sit by a fire. Hardly a need for coffee, or even breakfast.

Unconsciously meditating then, under the spell of a forty-mile solo journey through the mountains, I turned the corner of the trail and stopped short. A full-grown mountain lion was standing there in the trail, facing me, just a few lunges away. That great carnivore hunched its back in surprise, like a one hundred and fifty pound housecat. It was spring-loaded, deciding between fight and flight. It stared at me with big blue eyes that roughly matched the color of the sky.

At that moment, I wasn't afraid. Cougar attacks on people are rare, but they have happened. But I was hypnotized, excited to encounter one of the most difficult animals to find and to have enough time to enjoy it. This was no brief meeting. The cat was still looking me in the eyes. It wasn't until the third, or maybe even fourth second, before an instinctual fear started to stir my gut. After about five seconds of stalemate, I reluctantly raised my trekking poles into the air, which made me look like some strange, imposing creature, and I shouted, "YOU'RE BEAUTIFUL!"

After so many silent hours, the sound of my voice echoing back from the hillside startled me almost as much as it startled the mountain lion. The cat, god-like, disappeared out of sight as if wafting away into the air. I'd broken the spell of the wilderness.

After a moment, I walked over to where the cat had been. (I had to go that way, anyway.) All I could see was a series of uneven cliff edges and the steep, rolling hillsides below them covered, in short, dead grasses. The land seemed completely exposed, but the mountain lion, like the wolverine on Mount Holmes and the grizzly bears on Fawn Pass, had disappeared.

Then I was alone again, thirty miles down a forty-mile trail, standing on the remains of a fifty-million-year-old petrified redwood forest, looking for the ghost of a lion on the Sky Rim. I'd looked yet another of the continent's top-tier predators in the eyes, and yet again I'd been left to live another day. And I was living a life wholly unlike the one I'd always known.

It was September before I first saw the people that maintained the trails I'd been hiking all summer. Before that it hadn't even occurred to me that people were paid to work on trails. I'd walked across untold numbers of foot logs and bridges, and along trails held up with walls, but I hadn't thought about who'd built those structures.

Nathan and I were two-thirds through another thirty-mile loop, from Canyon Village to Lake Village and back through Pelican Valley. We were hiking together again. Our weekends still didn't perfectly match up, so we'd had to compress our trip into two nights instead of three. We were tired. But we only had two hours to walk the final ten miles to the trailhead if we were going to get to work on time.

That's when we stepped off the trail to let a group of four hikers pass us. They were marching fast on each other's heels, and they were all wearing orange helmets with the National Park Service arrowhead on the front. Two of them were carrying bright orange chainsaws on their shoulders.

We set out immediately in their footsteps. They were headed in the same direction as us, only they were making much better progress. "That's what *I* need to do," I said, gesturing toward the trail crew and breaking our silence. Nathan looked toward the top of the hill just as they were fading into the forest. He didn't say anything, but I knew he was thinking the same thing.

Higher Ground:
Old Men Don't Need Much Sleep

Richard LeBlond

I set out from Broken Bow, Nebraska, on the last day of spring 2011 to visit Wounded Knee on the Pine Ridge Indian Reservation in South Dakota. It was the third day of my annual trip west from North Carolina. I grew up in Oregon, but had moved east nearly 50 years before. Most of my family remained in the Portland area, and I flew out every Christmas. But when mom died in 2002, Christmas lost its cohesion, and I started driving out in summer. In addition to visiting family, I wanted to revisit places from my past and explore the unknown. Time had also become a factor. My bucket list had gotten more crowded without having to add new entries.

Wounded Knee is the site of an 1890 massacre of more than 150 Lakota Sioux men, women, and children. It is regarded by many historians as the final conflict for the West. The site has been designated a National Historic Landmark, but is not promoted for public visitation by U.S. or tribal authorities. There used to be a small village there with a trading post and museum, but these were destroyed in 1973 during an occupation by members of the American Indian Movement and consequent facedown with federal authorities.

In recent years, I have been reading more about the removal of Native Americans from their homelands, the forced settlement onto reservations, and the causes of conditions that persist on those reservations today. Books are dangerous. They awaken curiosity. They prompt journeys.

Since I regarded my visit as something close to trespass, I decided to bypass the reservation town of Pine Ridge, pay my respects quietly at the Wounded Knee cemetery, and leave unnoticed. As usual, things did not go as I imagined they would.

It was raining when I woke up in Broken Bow, and it rained all morning as I followed Route 2 through the green sandhills of northwestern Nebraska, the largest region of dunes in the Western Hemisphere. The unrelenting drizzle was becoming a threat to the outdoor lunch I had packed. On the road, I look for a natural setting for lunch, but if raining, I look for a restaurant. Skipping lunch was not an option. A life without lunch is a life without meaning.

By late morning, an indoor lunch appeared likely, and Pine Ridge was the only town around, about a dozen miles from the cemetery. It was still raining as I approached the reservation from Nebraska a little after eleven. I had been up since 5:30 and decided to have lunch before going to the cemetery. I was getting hungry, and it would give the rain another chance to realize it had made its point.

Barely two miles south of Pine Ridge, Nebraskans had a surprise waiting; the little border town of Whiteclay. It was unreal, like a movie set, exuding poverty, dilapidation, and lawlessness. Paint on some exterior walls — if there ever had been any — was gone. A few rough-hewn men entered and left small wooden buildings that otherwise would have appeared abandoned for decades. I wanted to stop and take a photo but was too scared. The road was narrow, the buildings and pedestrians close by. A balding and bearded man looked at me as if expecting a fight as he walked around the rubble of a disintegrating store front.

I later learned the little town was even worse than it looked. According to the 2008 documentary, *The Battle for Whiteclay,* this border town provides the vast majority of alcohol to the Pine Ridge Reservation, where sales and consumption are banned. According to the documentary's website:

> Since the early 1970s the State of Nebraska has licensed four off-sale beer retailers in Whiteclay. These retailers routinely violate Nebraska liquor law by selling beer to minors and intoxicated persons, knowingly selling to bootleggers who resell the beer on the reservation, permitting on-premise consumption of beer in violation of restrictions placed on off-sale-only licenses, and exchanging beer for sexual favors.[1]

Three years later, it appeared nothing had changed. The Whiteclay population of 14 is quite possibly the exact number it takes to run four beer stores and send contributions to those bureaucrats and politicians whose silence is crucial. Obviously, no public official is asking why a town of 14 people needs four beer retailers. The persistence of state-level corruption and abetted drug abuse — surely known by the Bureau of Indian Affairs — is strong evidence that at least one reprehensible 19th century practice remains inadmissible policy.

Getting to Pine Ridge was a relief, though there are few businesses in the small town, and it can't afford to hide its poverty. More than 80 percent of adult reservation residents are unemployed.

The only restaurants I saw as I drove the partially paved streets were Taco John's and a Subway. Then, unexpectedly, I saw a coffeehouse. It was tucked among trees on the main street and looked wildly out of place. Until then, I had associated coffeehouses with vibrant city life and trendy tourist destinations, not poverty-stricken towns on Indian reservations. I had been hanging out in coffeehouses since high school, and it was impossible for me to pass by what might be the beginning of a new world order.

---

1   battleforwhiteclay.org

I pulled into the small and informal parking area, walked among cared-for plants on the patio, and entered a small coffeehouse that would have been at home in any U.S. city. Its name was Higher Ground. Available coffees and pastries were neatly written on blackboards with chalk in the hippie tradition. Two women were working behind the counter, an older woman who appeared to be white, and a young Lakotan. When my turn came, I ordered a coffee and asked if they served lunch.

"Yes, we do," the older woman replied, "but it won't be ready for another hour or so. It's only 10:30."

I looked at my watch, which read 11:30, and realized I had entered the Mountain Time Zone.

"But I'm hungry," I mock-whined. "I woke up 4:30 your time in the Central Time Zone."

At that moment, a man's voice called out from the back of the seating area.

"Old men don't need much sleep."

I turned to see the source of this impertinence. He was a Lakotan, maybe in his mid-40s, with short hair, and wearing glasses. He was sitting at one of the small tables with a coffee and a laptop. There were only two other customers in the place, and our conversation continued across the room as I waited for my coffee.

"It's true I no longer need as much sleep," I said, taking him up on his invitation to a banter. "But I do need to eat. Even when I'm not hungry. On principle."

"Where are you from?"

"North Carolina."

"Cherokee?"

"White man."

"Why are you here?"

It was an astonishing interview. With nine words he had exposed our racial and ethnic divide. His tone was polite, and I was exhilarated as well as unsettled by his directness. The place and its history hold strangers to account, and his last question implied strangers never show up in Pine Ridge without an agenda. Mine was awfully small, but the time had come to declare it.

"To pay my respects at Wounded Knee." I had gotten about as far from "quietly ... leave unnoticed" as is possible.

Then, in a casual tone suggesting we had ended the "stranger" phase, he said, "When you get to the hill, walk up, don't drive. It will be a better experience."

Crossing the bridge he had built, I carried my coffee over to his table and remained standing.

"You're a writer," I guessed from familiarity with the habitat and its fauna.

"Well, I write. I wouldn't say I'm a writer."

"What are you working on?"

"I have a column in the local newspaper. It's due this afternoon but I've only just started working on it. I always wait until the last moment."

"I know the problem," I said. I used to write a newspaper column, and often waited until the day it was due. Some people are naturally inspired. Others must have it beaten out of them.

He introduced himself as Leon and said he had returned to the reservation after a successful business career in Minnesota. He told me he was drafting a book from his columns and blog site, was a part-time minister, and the cook at the coffeehouse. Leon was about to make my lunch.

His wife, not there at the time, was the coffeehouse boss, and the young Lakota woman behind the counter, their daughter. The two lunch specials that day were chicken with rice and Mongolian beef with Thai peppers. After Leon had finished cooking the two main courses, he brought his lunch as well as mine to my table. We had entered one of those lovely moments in life when two just-met people fit like old friends.

As we ate and talked, there was an older Lakota man, maybe my age, sitting at a nearby table. Occasionally, Leon would ask for his opinion or confirmation. The older man had long gray hair, well-worn clothes, few front teeth, and a quick smile. He looked like one of those chiefs in the old photographs. It was surreal, his sipping a designer coffee in a shop that could have been in Paris. I took it as a sign of hope, that he had come to Paris, and Paris to him.

The Grass of the Mass Grave

After lunch, I headed east from Pine Ridge for Wounded Knee. In spite of the rain and historical weight of my destination, I was still upbeat from my encounter with Leon at Higher Ground. Nine miles down the road was a "Wounded Knee" sign directing travelers left onto Big Foot Trail. But it didn't say how far to go, and it was the last "Wounded Knee" sign I would see. I eventually discovered that nothing marked the historical site beyond its physical presence as a small cemetery on a small hill in a sea of hills. Well, almost nothing.

Big Foot Trail followed a low ridge, passing through rolling grasslands dissected by a few wooded creeks. There were several scattered homes reflecting more than one rural income level. At one point, I saw a small dark brown building at the end of a short muddy road with a single word, "Museum," painted on the wall. I continued on for a few more miles until it seemed I had gone too far, and went back to see if there was anyone at the little museum. It wasn't much bigger than a car garage and about as plain.

As I drove up its road, I noticed a small cemetery on the hillock to the left. And suddenly there it was, the stone and ironwork arch I had remembered from the movies and documentaries, the entrance to the Wounded Knee cemetery. The lack of forewarning intensified the rush of recognition.

I pulled into the museum's muddy parking area. One other vehicle was in the lot, to my left, and as soon as I stopped, a young Lakota woman got out of it. Simultaneously, two young men stepped out from the darkness under the eave of the museum on my right. All three approached as I got out of the pickup, and didn't stop until they were within arm's reach. The woman was smiling, the two men looked dour, and I was apprehensive.

They reached into their pockets, and each pulled out a small and simple dreamcatcher, held flat in their outstretched palms. One of the men asked if I wanted to buy one, his tone bordering on sullen.

"Only $20. My wife is making them in the car." That seemed to eliminate them as museum employees, if there even was a museum. The little building was closed, and I later learned it had been closed for some time.

"No thanks," I said, feeling the annoyance that is my automatic response when I think I am being huckstered. "I bought all I'm going to buy today at the Heritage Museum in Pine Ridge," though what I spent there earned me precious little entitlement.

"You can make a donation," he said.

"I'll think about it," I said in my own sullen tone. Pulling away from them, I headed for the close-by cemetery and began my climb up the hill on foot, as Leon had recommended. But rather than the ascent being "a better experience," I had to deal with my negative response to what had happened in the parking lot. I could only be a stranger here, but I felt I held a stake in its terrible history, that its lessons were for all of us. So I was critical of what seemed an inappropriate use in a place of great meaning and significance. I would have paid a fee to the tribe for maintenance, protection, and interpretation of the site. But I had trouble accepting huckstering as a respectful use, and maybe the only protection — if you could call it that — the site was getting.

As I neared the top of the hill, I saw a younger Lakota man, maybe in his early twenties, standing next to the cemetery entrance. He was small, and had a striking face with sharp features, the face of a warrior, I thought. He introduced himself as Daniel, and I assumed correctly he was part of the team I had encountered in the parking lot. Conceding their superior number, I followed him through the entrance.

Daniel began recounting the history of the cemetery with a soft-spoken and dignified enthusiasm. He was so immediately likable that my mood began to brighten. I resolved to make a donation if he asked for it.

In the central portion of the cemetery, near the entrance, is a fenced-in area that is mostly mowed grass. Etched in the grass with a narrow cement line is a rectangle about 40 feet long and eight feet across.

Daniel tells me this is the outline of the mass grave for the more than 150 Lakota victims of the 1890 massacre.

Surrounding the fenced-in area are gravestones of people Daniel said had chosen to be buried there. He walked me to a stone monument located next to the mass grave about halfway down its length. The monument lists the names of some of the dead with a few details about what happened that snowy December day. It includes this statement: "Many innocent women and children who knew no wrong died here."

I had never been at a mass grave before. Just the thought of one is discomforting, and in its presence, I found myself enduring a suppression of emotion I hadn't experienced since pall-bearing my mother.

It has been proposed that Wounded Knee become a national monument. There is strong opposition to that notion by some on the reservation as paved parking lots and trails, entrance booths, gift shops, guided tours, and throngs of visitors would work against the solemnity of the site. Nonetheless, there is something to be said for rubbing Euro-American noses in the West's ethnic cleansings and genocides.

Daniel and I returned to the entrance arch. I asked him if the site of the massacre could be seen from where we stood. It was in open view directly below us. He explained in detail how the events had played out, where Big Foot's band of Lakotans had camped, how the Army had set up to contain them, and to where the Lakotans tried to flee when the shooting began.

Daniel tells the story with a disarming calmness. The lack of any stridency or emotional subjectivity keeps the listener close, attentive, and sympathetic. He lets the truth of this place tell itself.

I thanked him for the narrative. As I expected, he asked for a donation.

"I want to buy a new mower for the cemetery," he said.

I doubted his sincerity, but made a small donation anyway.

It was only on reflection, after I had returned home, that I realized someone had been mowing the grass of the mass grave. Doubtless it was Daniel. And the three young Lakotans in the parking lot — how long had they been waiting in the rain for the few wayfarers like myself? It was a miserable way to spend a day, and no one was going to make much money at a site that was almost invisible. After encountering them in the parking lot, I had viewed with disdain the probability that they and Daniel alone were providing the site its day-to-day care. I had not considered the commitment required, nor that they had an interest in the well-being of Wounded Knee during their tenure. And I'm certain at least one of them had a deeply-felt spiritual interest as well.

Now I wish I had bought one of the trinkets, as much for my mental health as for their profit. I could have hung it from the rearview mirror, where it might have caught a daydream.

Kicking the Snakes

Dawn S. Davies

Pain and drugs got me into graduate school. Not angst, mind you, but real, true, physical pain. The kind that makes your loved ones look at you with *that face,* the face that is part pity, part fear. The kind that makes them, quietly, when you aren't watching, hide the home defense goods: the oily, antique .380 handed down from a relative, the shotgun whose barrel is just long enough to reach your face if you put the butt of it on the ground and use a spatula to reach the trigger. I'm talking about the kind of pain that changes your worldview and makes you into a different person, and I'm talking about the kind of drugs doctors prescribe that ordinary people get hooked on all the time. The kind of drugs that, if you get hooked on them, will make you flush your own family down the toilet. Narcotics are no joke, but without experiencing an intolerable level of pain that required high doses of them, I would never have applied to graduate school. I am too anxious a person to do that kind of bold thing without artificial courage.

First, I need to explain something about anxiety. Some people get it in appropriate ways, under normal circumstances, say, right before public speaking or receiving some medical test results. Some people never experience it. My husband, for example, the rock that he is, says he has never felt "butterflies in his stomach" before an anxiety-provoking event. In fact, when I tried to talk about it with him, he said, "What's an anxiety provoking event?"

And there are some of us who get it far too often, whose bodies' fight or flight responses have been conditioned somehow, to be at Defcon 2 during the most common of events, such as waking up in the morning, or answering routine questions that employees at the DMV ask you. That's where I fall with anxiety. I don't know why I have it, but I do and it's awful. It's a joy sucker. I have tried anti-depressants, anti-anxiety medications, acupuncture, psychotherapy, homeopathy, herbs, rubber bands on my wrist, self-help books, prayer, hypnosis, divorce, biofeedback, neuro-feedback and other less easily defined techniques. None of these have worked, though it is kind of intriguing to pay twenty-four dollars for a *Bach Flower Remedy* that goes down like a gimlet and makes you feel like have been duped in a wooden-wagon, medicine show kind of way. The ten minutes of hope is worth the money.

Anxiety forces you to live a double life. It immediately splits you in two parts, mind and body. Your mind escorted into a big warehouse of unreality, where the worst what-ifs you can imagine, the most absurd things that will most likely never come true, are stored for just in case, so if one of them ever happens, you can tell yourself "I told you so." There are things in there like tumors, falling out of an airplane, car accidents, inopportune public burping, aortic aneurysms, home invasion, widowhood, chemo recliners, ALS. Your body is left behind to fake it to friends and family and co-workers, often thumping with a parasympathetic frenzy, causing you to sweat, forcing your adrenal glands to squirt out adrenaline to the point where your face and hands feel numb and your blood pressure drops until you need to sit down from the dizziness. You can't interact honestly with those around you when your mind is in the warehouse of useless what-ifs, and your body thinks it is having a heart attack.

I cannot count how many times I sat with a friend or family member, pretending to listen to them talk about something that was important to them, nodding my head, but secretly not giving one shit, because my internal self was trying to swallow down a fear of ovarian cancer being discovered at my upcoming routine checkup, or a worry that my daughter was going to get abducted by a stranger on the way home from school, or regret over something wrong I had said to one of my stepsons. These are the things that, because you can't share them with anyone, cause you to split yourself and live a lie.

There's more: I have two autoimmune diseases and I suspect that chronic, unrelenting anxiety has contributed to this state, because anxiety can unbalance the hormonal system, which can lead to disease, et cetera and like the classic causality dilemma, I have wondered which came first; my chicken of a mind, or the raw, busted egg of my autoimmune disease.

When you sit autoimmune disease next to anxiety, the two will goad and poke at each other like siblings in the backseat of a small car on a long road trip. Stop touching me. You did it first. Shut up or I'll tell Mom. Get off my side. The line is here. No, let me draw the line. You're *touching* the line. You don't know what you're doing. That's not the middle. *Stop touching me.* Fine, give me back my headphones, then, and so on. As a parent of real children, you can lay down the law any time you want. You can pull over the car and open up a can of whoop-ass that is so excellent the children will regret acknowledging the other's presence. The rest of the ride will be as sweet and as quiet as if you were alone. If you are very good, they will never fight in the car again. But as the guardian of autoimmune disease processes and chronic anxiety, punishing myself won't make my mind-body behave. I have to wheedle. Con, nag, manipulate. Resort to desperate measures.

I had wanted to be a writer for a long time, and I kind of was. I wrote web content for a few different companies. I developed courses for online high school and college programs. I wrote a few academic children's books, and advertising copy for a publishing house, most of this from the anxiety-reducing comfort of my own home, but what I secretly wanted to do was the kind of study that would lead me to an MFA in creative writing. I thought that by getting an MFA I would become, with the same earnest desire as Pinocchio, a *real writer*. I wanted to let my soul free to write the things I wanted to write. Though, really, I apologize for even talking about this because there is nothing more annoying to me than writers writing about writing, especially writers writing about how writing makes "the soul sing." Seriously, if I could bring myself to get on an airplane, I would rather sit in front of a seat-kicking kid with an ear infection for the entirety of a transatlantic flight than read or write about writers who write about writing. But there it is, my soul-singing desire, spit up like a fur ball, and when I tell you I wanted it badly, I mean it.

There was an MFA program that I had my eye on. Every year, for perhaps six years, I would print out an application, fill it out, prepare a writing sample, be overcome with anxiety, and throw the application away. I could imagine a panel of people passing my manuscript around and shaking their head, their noses squinched slightly, politely, as if someone else in the room had just farted the kind of fart that comes after eating Thai food. I could imagine getting the form letter rejection, saying that the competition was particularly tough that year and they had many qualified applicants and only a few slots, et cetera. I knew that rejection came with writing, but I couldn't face the kind pre-rejection, that uber rejection that I might not be good enough to even get *into* a writing program.

When I finally got up the courage to apply, I was crunked out on drugs, which was necessary. Here's how I did it: I went surfing on a windy day. I let the surfboard act as a sail and rip my right shoulder back, tearing my labrum somewhere deep inside the socket. It hurt and weakened my shoulder, but because I wasn't enthusiastic about having surgery, I walked around like that for a year before getting up the guts to have it fixed. I had not been told that the recovery for this kind of surgery is incredibly painful, so much so that you can't sleep lying down for several weeks. You have to sleep in a chair. A surgeon will not tell his patients how bad a recovery will be, because if he did, no one would ever schedule a surgery. They would just walk around all third-worldly, wearing slings and limping and popping pills and keeling over now and then, and surgeons would be renting apartments like the rest of us. I had a urologist who admitted this to me once, so I know it's true.

I had developed a kidney stone a few years back, which is not that uncommon, especially for me, though every time I get one, it is the worst pain I have ever experienced and my husband gives me *the face* and hides the home defense equipment. Kidney stones are demonic, excruciating, worse than childbirth and twenty other clichés about pain that would allow for an et cetera here, and apparently, though I walk the planet like an Amazon, I have tiny, delicate, shrinking violet ureters which are not big enough in diameter to pass even a tiny stone. So every stone I develop gets repeatedly stuck trying to go down the water flume and slams itself, over and over, into the entrance to my ureter, like trying to shove a golf ball through a garden hose. This creates the kind of pain that if left alone on, say, a high bridge with a spread of sharp rocks beneath it, and an angry, cold current, it might make you jump off. Without surgery for even these tiny stones, I would probably die from some sort of infection or a backing up of the pipes.

When I get a kidney stone, I require the placement of a cruel device called a ureteral stent, which a doctor will tell you is a soft, malleable harmless piece of plastic, but which is actually a tube with two coiled springs, one that sits lodged inside your kidney and one that floats around in your bladder. The tube that connects the kidney end to the bladder end helps keep the ureter from closing due to inflammation or scar tissue, and, if all goes well, allows the stone to pass. The bladder end of the stent is attached to a string which comes out your very sensitive flower of a pee hole and gets taped to your thigh. Stents themselves are terribly painful, and for me, cause nearly unbearable bladder and ureter spasms, sometimes just when I switch positions in a chair. They are so bad I can't sleep. Every time I feel a spasm, it makes me groan and weep loudly. I can't get through one without waking my husband up at night, or if it is in the daytime, without making people come running into the room, even though I don't want to bother anybody. I usually keep a stent in for nine days or so, just long enough for me to feel defeated about humanity, and all of this requires copious levels of narcotics just to get through it. And when the stent is out, and the pain eventually ebbs away, I must get myself off of the narcotics, which I grow to enjoy taking.

In order to remove a stent, the doctor grabs ahold of the string, lies through his teeth about how much it will hurt, and yanks the stent out like he is hauling up a lobster trap. The spring leaves your kidney and travels down your ureter and out your urethra. They don't tell you how this is going to feel. There are no words, and besides, if people knew, they wouldn't come back to the office to have their stents removed. They would avoid it at all costs, walking around all third-worldly, until they keel over and die from the stent growing into their tissue and backing things up all over again.

I believe there is a level of fundamental purity you maintain, no matter how tainted you are by pornography, or crime, or cruelty, or poverty, or violence, when you haven't experienced a certain level of pain, or perhaps war. I believe there are some people able to avoid it for a lifetime, careful people, or lucky ones, or people with congenital analgesia, who walk around with this type of innocence, and it is a rare gift. Though I have had three babies three separate times without anesthesia, which does sting the hoo-ha mightily, the day I go to have my first stent removed is the last day of my true innocence. The doctor, whose name is Khan, as in Ghengis, I kid you not, greets us like he had just had a good weekend.

He is tan and rested and acts like he wants to get this over with because there is a nice club sandwich, or maybe a high class call girl waiting on his desk in his office. He shakes hands with my husband. I have worn a skirt so I wouldn't have to change into a paper robe, so I lay back on the table and hike it up self-consciously, in front of this slightly wolfish man, while my husband watches.

"This might sting a little bit," he says.

"What do you mean sting?" I ask.

"I mean you might feel a little pinch."

"Okay," I go. "Whatever. I'm just ready to get this thing out." I am not worried at this point, because I am an innocent, an innocent doped up on narcotics. While we are talking the doctor spreads my legs and aims a bright light on my hoo-ha.

"You might want to hold her hand," he tells my husband. "Here we go." He rips the tape off of my thigh, causing me to remark, in my innocence, "Wow, that *did* sting," and then grabs the string and starts pulling the stent out, the coil stretching out and putting pressure against the tender things that should never be touched by anything, pressing against my ureter, and out my violated urethra. This takes perhaps seven seconds, but in those seven seconds, the universe implodes behind my eyes. I see the corruption of all mankind, Adam raping Eve in the garden, children suffocating puppies, my grandparents wading through a landscape of vomit, snakes and skulls, Aretha Franklin's backup singers humming generations of lies brought to life in an echo of falsetto. My eyes roll back in my head and I nearly lose consciousness. There is a white sheet in my field of vision and I start crying hard.

"You sonofabitch!" I shriek. "That wasn't a pinch! You are a damn liar!"

"They always do this," he says to my husband. "I have to lie. If I told you how bad it was, you would have worried about it. But now it's over." He peels off his gloves, turning his back to face the sink, which is when I first realized that doctors lie, and also, that life is very, very short. It got me thinking about all the things I had been too afraid to do, but should have, because stupid things like war or infection or crank-ass random accidents can finish people off without them doing what they were put here to do. That one stent was enough pain for a lifetime.

So, when it was time to have my shoulder repaired, I was uneasy enough to want to get the truth out of the orthopedic surgeon.

"What's the pain level going to be like after this?"

"You'll be uncomfortable."

"How uncomfortable? Because usually when you guys say 'uncomfortable' it means I end up crying."

"It's a surgical procedure. You're going to be uncomfortable, but I'm going to give you pain medication, so you'll be fine."

"So, some pain meds and I'll be fine?"

"Look. Everything has a price. You're an active girl. You want the shoulder fixed for the rest of your life, you're going to have go through a little discomfort."

I wake up from surgery with blood all over my face. It is dripping down from my eyes, down my cheeks and into my neck. I am in excruciating pain, right out of the gate. I hear a voice.

"How's the discomfort, sweetie? Give me a number from one to ten." It is the recovery nurse.

"Eleven," I whisper. "My face is bleeding. Why is my face bleeding?"

"It's tears, sweetie. You're crying. I've never seen anyone wake up crying from surgery before. Congratulations, you get morphine." This would be my last year of crying, of real tears leaking from my eyes, though I didn't know it then.

So, I go home that day with a prescription for some hardcore narcotic pain medication and Ambien, a powerful sleeping pill.

"Trust me," the nurse says. "You're gonna need these. Patients who have this surgery find it difficult to sleep for a long time."

"I think the doctor lied again," I say to my husband on the way home.

I didn't sleep more than four hours a night for the next two months. I would take an Ambien around nine, fall fitfully asleep and dream of monsters, things with triangular teeth in red, angry gums biting me, only the teeth were loose, they stuck in my skin, left a poison in my shoulder that streaked red, up to my brain. Or I would dream of being led on a tour around a gracious old house, when all I really wanted was the bathroom, opening door after door, looking into closets, bedrooms, studies, libraries, shops, and finally seeing a door marked toilet and opening it to find one of those dreaded windy air bendy giant nylon sock people that used car dealers put in front of their lots popping out at me, making me wet my pants in front of the dangerous, desperate president of an economically unstable nation. It was his house that I was touring, I had found out just that second, and I was some sort of ambassador. A lot rode on how I carried myself through this tour.

I would wake up to pain, soaked with pain-induced sweat, yet be unable to change my nightgown because my shoulder hurt so much that I couldn't dress myself. I would ease myself out of the recliner I slept in, take more narcotics and walk around like a ghost in my wet nighty, billowing it around me until it dried out, sitting on a chair for a few minutes, then when the pain got too bad, moving to the couch to watch infomercials until the meds kicked in, then up for some laps around the dining room table, then outside on the front porch, then back inside to wrap a Christmas present with one hand, then over to the computer to surf for something to distract me. Anything to keep moving, because sitting still is what made the pain build until it made me cry. I did this for weeks.

There are two things to mention about narcotics here. The first is that, like post-surgery shoulder pain, the strength and power of narcotics should not be underestimated. I am sensitive to drugs of all kinds, and I don't like them at all. I don't even drink alcohol. I can taste in my mouth the moment when Tylenol hits my system. I have uncommon, often severe side effects to medications and prefer to not take them, and still I was sucked in to the allure of narcotics. They do something to the brain that makes you crave them, and once you no longer need the drugs, you still want them. You love them, and you want to be loved by them, so your brain tells you that you must have them.

Another thing is that narcotics are the only things I have found, to date, that have taken away my anxiety. On Percocet, I did not give one flying fart about what anyone thought about me. I did not over-examine the things I said or did, and I stopped worrying about things that would never happen. I became a different, more neurotypical person when I was taking them, and I loved every bit of how they made me feel. I could think about driving to the grocery store without getting a knot in my stomach. I could answer the telephone without butterflies. I could think about my kids growing up without imagining them getting leukemia. I could think of my daughters' wedding days without imagining myself dead. Narcotics did what Valium and Xanax and Bach Flower Remedies and homeopathy and psychotherapy had never been able to do. They hobbled my personality, but made me, in a way, into a better, more functional person. The only anxiety I felt was when I thought about living without them.

One night just before Christmas, when the rest of the house was sleeping and I was desperate for distraction, I went online and checked the MFA program deadline and realized I had just a few weeks left if I wanted to apply. I was plotzed out of my gourd during this time, feeling nothing but pain, and what a relief it was. I mean, it was so good to not worry about ridiculous things, or of having an anxiety attack while sitting alone on the back porch with a magazine. I printed out the application and made a checklist of things I needed to do to apply. Then, for the rest of the week, in fifteen minute increments while my family was sleeping, I worked on my application until it was done. I was unapologetically, heavily shit-canned during the whole process, including writing the sample of my work, but my nerves were Rico Suave, sitting at a bar wearing a Panama hat and vest with a pocket watch, drinking Southern Comfort Manhattans. I mailed the application without fear, and then I waited.

During the three months of waiting, I had started to scare myself when I realized that I was looking forward to each dose of Percocet, and I loved the fifteen minute high the Ambien gave me right before I fell asleep. I thought I might be in trouble when, after a hard day, I took an extra pill just to feel better emotionally, and it worked. Then I did it again the next day just to see if I was right. Then I started taking two per dose and then I started taking a second Ambien in the middle of the night.

To steal a phrase, *everything was beautiful and nothing hurt.* There was no pain and there was no anxiety.

We all know how pill heads ruin their lives. We have all heard the stories of normal people, schoolteachers, or bank managers or housewives, et cetera, who get in a car accident and start taking Percocet and muscle relaxants, and end up crushing and snorting black market oxys on the back of strangers' toilets, or giving blowjobs in exchange for pills, losing their jobs and their families in the process of the decline. Talk to any police officer and he will tell you that pill heads are dangerously numb — empty zombies who operate with the singular goal of obtaining more pills. And don't let them lie to you; the sleeping medication Ambien is highly addictive. When taken together, Ambien and Percocet make even a common, garden-variety housewife panic when she thinks the prescriptions might be getting low, or worse, that there are no refills left, and worse yet, leads her to ruminating on some experimental ideas, such as how far one could go to get more of these drugs when the prescription runs out. Sell the wedding ring? Dip into savings? Leave the children home alone to go meet some guy named "Toothless" in an IHOP parking lot?

At this point, I didn't technically need the drugs anymore, but I wanted them terribly. I liked how I felt just a little numb, numbed up enough to not feel the worry that had dominated my personality for most of my life. I knew I was treading in dangerous water, the kind of water with a big undertow that was just waiting for me to go to the doctor and fib about my pain levels, or find an ER resident I could lie to about back pain, an undertow that was just waiting for me to hide a bottle of pills from my husband, or hide an addiction from myself. One Friday night, at about eleven, after the kids were asleep, I grabbed my pills and took them to my husband, who was reading in bed. I handed him the bottles.

"I need to stage my own intervention. I'm getting too dependent on these."

"Okay," he said slowly.

"You know I have an addictive personality."

"You do."

"I need to stop these now," I said. I was embarrassed to admit this kind of weakness, especially to a man who, besides a small, nagging issue with Monster Energy Drinks, doesn't even have a vice.

And here is part of the beauty of my husband. He got out of bed, grabbed the bottles of pills, took me by the elbow and led me to the bathroom. He handed me a bottle.

"Open it," he said. I did. "Now flush it." I did. He handed me the other one, and I dumped it and flushed, drugging fish and other wildlife all over Southeast Florida.

"Are there refills on these?" he asked.

"One on each."

"Give me the bottles," he said. I handed them to him and he put them in his pocket so I wouldn't be able to use the prescription number to call in a refill.

"Thank you for telling me," he said.

"You're welcome," I said, and this is another beautiful thing about my husband, his ability to allow me to feel generous and beneficent as a result of things he does.

It took me weeks to get back to a normal sleeping pattern without the drugs, and within a few days of quitting, the anxiety started creeping back up past Defcon 4, to Defcon 3, and finally, Defcon 2, where I could hear my own heart beating in my ears as a matter of course and push myself into an anxiety spiral simply by poking my imagination, and I realized, very clearly, very cleanly, in an unimpaired way, that I had applied to graduate school while I was on drugs.

Around the end of March, a few weeks after flushing my drugs, I began to feel queasy in the hours before the mailman delivered the mail each day, or when I opened up my email in the morning. I began to check the school website several times per day, the mailbox on my porch several times per day, and my email several times per day. When I thought about the MFA program, I would sometimes get nervous diarrhea, which led me to fool myself into believing I didn't want to get in after all, that MFA degrees did not matter. The market was flooded with baristas and middle school tutors with MFAs behind their names, and besides, I had important things going on at home. There were some soffits that needed scraping and repainting. I was thinking about starting to sew the kids' clothes again, because they were in high school and the fashions were more challenging. I had also watched an internet video on how to paint a faux mahogany look on a garage door and I had it in mind to do it. Maybe I would even start a home business offering faux wood garage door painting to people in wealthier neighborhoods. I told myself I put the program out of my mind, but I couldn't. I wanted it too much.

The thing that drug abuse and anxiety and pain flirt with, bat back and forth like a badminton birdie, a themed and crocheted hacky sack, a psychological hot potato, is *loss of control*. Nobody wants to lose control. Nobody wants to give it up. Before I had my first child, the thing I was afraid of more than the pain of natural childbirth was accidentally having a bowel movement in front of the midwife while I was pushing. And now, years later, when I think of the pain, I can't remember its particulars, but I do recall shitting myself while pushing, and the midwife wiping my bottom with a Chux, saying, "Oopsie, a little poopsie!"

So we develop anxiety to brace ourselves for adjustments we are afraid to make due to things we don't want to happen. We develop hypochondriasis in anticipation of the ultimate loss of control — death. We drink at parties so we can control how we are viewed, so we can be seen by others as interesting and entertaining. We avoid pain because we fear it becoming worse, unbearable even, to where we want to jump off a bridge or shoot ourselves in the heads to make it stop. We take drugs to protectively numb ourselves from an accumulation of lifelong pain of all sorts — physical, psychological and psychic. These things, especially when they work in concert, weave in and out of each other. We take drugs to avoid pain, we avoid pain because we are afraid of losing control, and we lose control trying to not feel pain. The pain eats the drugs, the drugs eat the anxiety, the anxiety eats the pain and we are left with a roil of snakes shaped like a Celtic knot, each with another's tail in its dirty little mouth. Everything has a price.

Sometimes, perhaps even for one day, during that fresh, drug-free, post-surgical state, when my pain was improved, and my shoulder injury was healing, I felt a tiny bit of control that came on me of its own volition. It wasn't drug induced. It felt hopeful — there wasn't an anticipation of pain in my immediate future, save the possible rejection from the MFA program, and honestly, fuck them, right? Who were they to tell me I would or wouldn't "be" a writer? I was feeling a little giddy, a little silly in the way that someone who just cheated death feels, so the kids and I planned an April Fool's Day prank on my husband. I curled up on my bed. The kids ran out to get my husband, who was outside doing something manly that it would have been inconvenient to stop, like digging a fence-post hole. They said, "Something's wrong with Mommy. You have to come inside." I waited, curled on the bed, snickering inside my armpit. When I heard his footsteps on the bedroom floor, I groaned.

"I think I have a kidney stone," I said.

"You're kidding me." I got up and paced across the room bent over, yet on tiptoes, the way I walk when I have a kidney stone. I groaned again like a goat, my kidney pain sound.

"Jeezy Petes," he said. "Looks like we're going to the ER," and this is where we burst out laughing, shouting "April Fools! Ha ha! We fooled you, didn't we?" My husband, who doesn't generally appreciate pranks, wasn't amused.

The next morning, in the ultimate payback, I woke up with a real kidney stone. We drove to the ER where I vomited on the floor and passed out, while the tiny stone slammed against my ureter, trying to escape. They admitted me. I had surgery. They gave me another stent. When I woke up pissing iron filings and razor blades, filling the toilet with blood, they mercifully whacked me out of my skull with a morphine drip. My husband had brought my laptop, and I was able to fool around on it between the hallucinations I had of Chinese men with Fu Manchu moustaches floating down from the ceiling, lips a' pucker, to kiss me about the face and neck. I checked my email and found one from director of the

MFA program telling me I was accepted for the following fall with full funding. In fact, thanks to the morphine and another prescription bottle of hydrocodone, I don't remember my hospital stay, I don't remember the nurses, and I usually make friends with the nurses. I don't remember my doctor, and I don't remember opening that email and getting one of the best pieces of news of my life.

But when faced with a new thing, we always get a choice. We can turn back to what we know is safe and comfortable, or we can take a chance and do the thing, even if it scares us. I got out of the hospital, had my stent removed, and this time, when I stopped needing the drugs for pain control, I stopped taking them. I kicked the knot of snakes into the dirt and instead of looking forward to an imagined, always apocalyptic personal future, I looked forward to something real that was actually going to happen. It was a baby step of a difference, this glimmer of a change in thinking, this little truth in an otherwise hypochondriacal soap opera, yet it made a difference, gave me a bit of focus, made my soul sing, et cetera.

Reflection

Corinne Sullivan

Invasion

There lives in New Guinea a tribe called the Biami who, until somewhat recently, never knew the existence of mirrors. A few Biami men used mirror shards to reflect light, but the shards were too small for the men to really see themselves in. They have no standing bodies of water in which to see their reflections. When anthropologists introduced full-body mirrors to this isolated tribe, their immediate reaction was paralyzed fear. They covered their mouths, ducked their heads, and stood transfixed, staring at the images before them. Terror of self-awareness, the anthropologists called it.

You, too, once lived in this mirror-less Eden. Sure, you used mirrors to inspect the hole left in your mouth after you fell off the monkey bars at recess and lost your first tooth, or to pin back your bangs when you were growing them out in third grade. But it isn't until that ski weekend at Smuggler's Notch that you and Meredith went on when you were fourteen, when you put on your bikini to go in the hot tub and Meredith said, holy shit, look at your abs, that you even became aware that you had a body, and a body worthy of praise at that. Abs? You had always associated those with beefy weightlifters, the ones who would hang out in gyms grunting and sweating and lifting barbells until their arms were sinewy and their stomachs were rippled and tight. How could *you* have them? You stood before the mirror sucking in your stomach, turning from side to side. You couldn't see what Meredith seemed to see but you saw the envy in her eyes; that had been impossible to miss.

Up until a certain point in your life there had only been Fat and Skinny, and you carried with you the knowledge that you were Skinny. When the soccer coach handed out uniforms, you knew you would get one of the smallest ones. When you played games of Chicken Fight in Meredith's pool, you knew people would argue over who got to have you on their shoulders. When you mixed Hoodsie cups and Oreos and Chocolate Poptarts and chocolate sauce in a blender and then drank it all up and your mom said if you kept that up you'd have to be rolled around everywhere you went, you actually laughed at the thought — you, Fat! Impossible! Age had made you aware of your body, aware of yourself, but this self-awareness only made you believe that, when it came to your body, you had nothing to worry.

Then you go to college.

Complication

Studies find that the presence of a mirror in a room changes human behavior, often in surprisingly industrious ways. Subjects tested in a room with a mirror are found to work harder, to be more helpful, and are less likely to cheat as compared to control groups tested in non-mirrored settings. Likewise, people in a room with a mirror are comparatively less inclined to cast judgment on others based on social stereotypes such as sex, race, or religion. The mirror has a sort of panoptical effect, with the constant threat of being on display forcing one into intensified self-awareness.

When they can see their reflection, people tend to eat less, too.

You don't feel the effects of the college campus Panopticon immediately. When you become a member of the school's dance team and don your new uniform for the first time, a cropped shell top that leaves your midriff bare and tight black pants, your roommates stare. I don't know how you can wear that thing in front of the whole school, they say, while you think, why wouldn't you be able to? After all, you're irrefutably Skinny, aren't you? When you go to eat an ice cream cookie sandwich after dinner and the older girls on the dance team say they used to eat shit like that before they realized how many calories it had, you check the package and see that that it has 420 calories. Is that a lot? You're not even sure.

And then there's Nikki on the dance team, Nikki, who is always running laps before practice and eating weird stuff like chickpeas and cottage cheese for dinner, the one that everyone in the stands is always pointing at during football games. Look at her body, they say. They would kill to have her body. But you don't understand. You're both Skinny. So why is no one in the stands pointing at you?

Back in your room, you confront your reflection. You lift up your shirt, suck in your stomach, turn your body from side to side. You open up *Women's Health*. Jessica Alba smiles in a bikini, her flesh like plastic wrap stretched over a dish. You look back up at your reflection. You, you are soft. You run your hands over your stomach, your hips — when did you even get hips? You pinch your skin between your fingers, pretending you're made of clay. Clay that you have the power to mold into anything that you'd like.

Fixation

Self-awareness once frightened the Biami tribe members, but within a matter of days they were observed grooming themselves openly before their new mirrors. Once they saw themselves for what they were, how could they resist? No longer were their bodies simply physical extensions of themselves, carrying them as they blundered and bobbled through space; that flesh, they realized, was their responsibility, to adorn and to groom and to shape. To perfect. Self-awareness had made the Biami prisoners to the reflections before them.

You start going to the gym. You run, you squat, you lift, you press, you sweat. You start to pay close attention to parts of your body that you had never even considered before: the indentation in your forearms where muscle is starting to build, the sharp definition in your calves, the dimples in your lower back (you had thought this last feature was cause for concern until you had done some research on the Internet and discovered that men find back dimples, or Dimples of Venus, as they are known, very sexy). In the dance studio, on the stationary bike, lifting free weights, you're rapt by the figure in the mirror before you, the one whose body was once soft and svelte like a child's, Skinny but nothing special, that you have shaped with your own hands into this lean, muscular creature, all sharp lines and angles. You turn your back to the mirror and flex, watching all these new muscles rippling through your back. You can't take your eyes off yourself.

It's not enough. They all still point at Nikki and say look at her body, but no one is pointing and looking at you. That's because Nikki is now running laps before *and* after practice, and eating just cottage cheese. Make sure you're working out and eating healthy, your dance team coach is always saying, because she wants you all to be your Best Selves. You all know what she is really saying: she wants you all to be Skinnier. You begin to ask yourself, do you really need that cheese on your sandwich? That's an extra hundred calories you could cut out every day. And cookies, ice cream? No more of that. Cheerios, dry chicken breasts, salads with light fat-free dressing. You stand before the mirror, lift up your shirt, turn from side to side. You want collarbones that pop out of your chest, shoulder blades so sharp they look like they might puncture your skin, a stomach so emaciated that there isn't an inch of flesh to hold on to. You want people to want to kill for a body like yours.

Obligation

Panopticism was inspired by a model prison with a radial configuration in which the prisoners couldn't see the inspector who watched from within. Because the prisoner could never know when he was being inspected, uncertainty could be used as an instrument of discipline. Once the inmates were induced into a state of conscious and perpetual visibility, automatic functioning of power was guaranteed. Surveillance was permanent in its effects, even if it is discontinuous in its actions. The inmates were trapped in a power situation, a perpetual two-way mirror, of which they themselves were the bearers.

You can't pass a mirror, a window, a single reflective surface without stalling, staring, turning from side to side, studying your figure. You are Narcissus, gazing into a pool at your own reflection, and yet this habit becomes so frequent that the reflection begins to feel like somebody else. This isn't your body, the one that has carried you through twenty years of life, the body that has allowed you to turn cartwheels and swim laps and climb trees; it is an entirely separate entity that you have been given the responsibility to perfect. *Fit* is no longer gratifying; you want the image looking back at you to conjure the words *waiflike, bony, gaunt*. You squeeze your flesh in frustration, as if it really is malleable in your hands, as if you could simply mold your body into that sharp, angular, curveless physique that you just can't seem to attain.

Distortion

Two psychologists once designed an experiment with a body-distorting mirror that could be adjusted to create various convex or concave reflections. The subjects stood before the mirror, watching their reflections morph from tall and elongated to short and compressed. Then, when the subjects were asked to adjust it themselves to restore their normal reflection, they struggled. Many of them forgot, after seeing such distorted perceptions of themselves, what they actually looked like. What was actually normal.

Flesh sickens you. Paunchy bellies, flabby thighs, wide hips, soft curves: they all make you stare in revulsion. You're not sure if everyone else has always been this Fat, or if you're just now starting to notice it. They make you want to work even harder so that you may be that much slighter and bonier in comparison. You watch the new girls on the dance team eating their pizza and fries; disgusting, you think. Didn't they hear about the marketing director approaching the dance team coach, how he said these girls aren't Skinny enough, these girls need to be Skinnier? Don't these new girls care about being their Best Selves? You tell the girls that you used to eat shit like that before you realized how many calories everything had. You barely even remember what it feels like to enjoy food; now everything you eat makes you queasy with regret, sitting in your stomach like a viscous rock. Part of you hopes that these others girls will just continue to eat and eat and eat so you become increasingly smaller and thinner and bonier in comparison, while another part wishes that food would afflict them with the same incapacitating, maddening guilt that it afflicts you, so that you wouldn't feel so alone.

But you're not alone. Every girl pumping away on the ellipticals in the gym, trying to push herself harder, to stay on for longer, telling herself you need to stay on for twenty minutes longer because you ate that Oreo after dinner last night (why did you eat that Oreo anyway? Did you really need that Oreo?) and you need to get those Oreo calories out of your body, every girl beating herself up for not going to kickboxing class on Tuesday night because she had wanted to watch a *TV* show with her roommates instead but now can't stop thinking about all those calories she didn't burn, every girl debating between two granola bars because one is 110 calories and one is 125 calories because even though she prefers the brand that has the 125 calories, the fifteen calories suddenly seems incredibly significant, every girl sweating and starving and shrinking and shriveling and drifting around campus seeking out all the girls who are still Skinnier than she is, all those withered corpses of girls whose slight, emaciated figures seem to mock her, because she doesn't have the discipline, the willpower, the commitment to being as Skinny as them: every one of them is you. They're all outward manifestations of your own fixation. You find yourself staring into hundreds of different mirrors, all of you challenging one another to be Skinnier, Skinnier, Skinnier except, to you, they're all succeeding. And then there's you, looking at your own reflection in the mirror, realizing that you're never going to be Skinny enough.

Delusion

Mirrored-Self Misidentification is a condition characterized by the inability to recognize one's own reflected image. The afflicted believe that the reflection they see in the mirror is not their own, but another person, even a stranger following them around. People who suffer from this are usually split into one of two groups: either a person has lost the ability to interact properly with mirrors, or the person has somehow lost the ability to recognize his or her own face.

You talk to your reflection. You need to lose weight, you tell it. You're Fat.

It stares back at you. You are disgusted by it.

Enervation

As mirrors gradually penetrated the island of New Guinea, natives who had never before known the presence of mirrors reacted similarly to how the Biami had. When the Motumotu on the southern coast first saw their likenesses in a mirror, they thought these reflections were their souls. The notion that mankind possesses a symbolic self in addition to his physical self is universal, yet the mirror reveals more: a symbolic self *outside* the physical self. Placed before a mirror, that symbolic self, once private and sacred, is suddenly explicit, public, vulnerable. Open to scrutiny. To judgment. Needing to be controlled and maintained, even outside the immediate eye of surveillance.

You stop getting your period. Your hair falls out in clumps. You pin sheets over all the mirrors in your apartment, as the doctor recommended, but when your roommates aren't home, you move the sheets aside and return to the mirror.

You suck in your stomach. You turn from side to side. You're not even sure what it is you're looking for anymore.

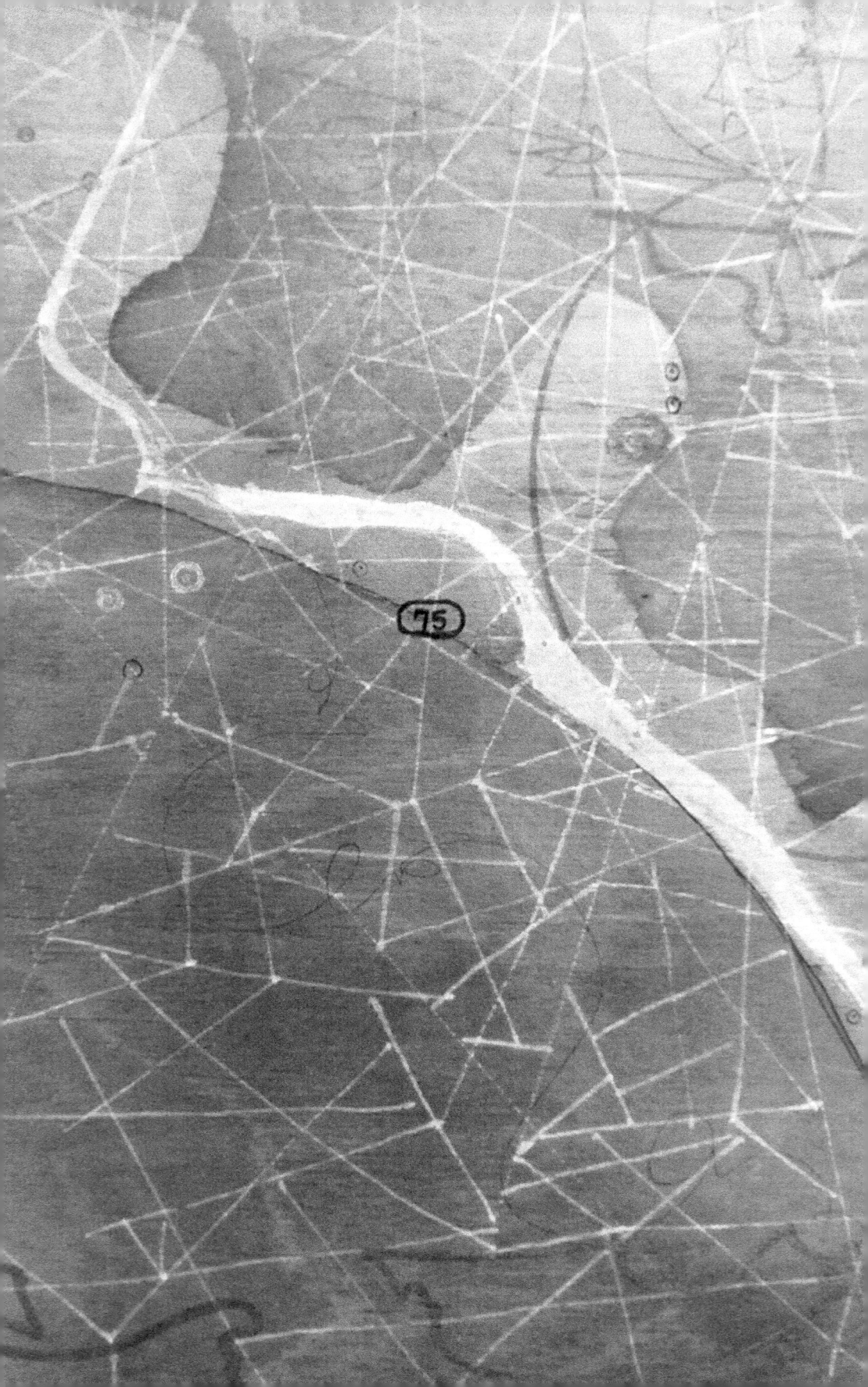

ABOUT THE CONTRIBUTORS

Poetry

Lana Bella

Lana Bella has a diverse work of poetry and flash fiction published and forthcoming with *Anak Sastra, Atlas Poetica, Bewildering Stories, Calliope Magazine, Eunoia Review, Cecil's Writers' Magazine, Deltona Howl, Earl of Plaid Lit, Family Travel Haiku, First Literary Review-East, Foliate Oak Literary, Garbanzo Literary Journal, Global Poetry, Ken*Again, Marco Polo Arts Literary, Nature Writing, The Commonline Journal, The Higgs Weldon, The Voices Project, War Anthology: We Go On, Thought Notebook, Undertow Tanka Review, Wordpool Press, Wilderness House Literary Review, Featured Artist with Quail Bell Magazine,* and now, *New Plains Review.* She resides on some distant isle with her novelist husband and two frolicsome imps.

Clayton Adam Clark

Clayton Adam Clark lives in St. Louis, Missouri, his hometown, where he communicates and fundraises for one of the largest eye banks in the country. He earned the MFA in poetry at Ohio State University and is currently working on his first poetry collection. Some of his other poems are forthcoming in *Southern California Review, Southern Humanities Review, Bellingham Review,* and elsewhere.

Jonathan Cooper

Jonathan's essays have appeared in a number of publications including *The Statesman Journal* and *The Vancouver Sun,* and his poem 'Downpour' will appear in a forthcoming edition of *Radix Magazine.* He lives with his wife and son in Vancouver, Canada, where he works in the real estate business.

Benedict Downing

Benedict Downing has written fiction, poetry since adolescence. He joined local community reading circles, workshops, and college literary groups. Writes fiction and poetry for literary journals and magazines. There are two published books written by Mr Downing, a poetry book, "Sidereal Reflux" (2011), and a novel, "Epicrisis" (2014). He is currently working on his second novel.

Addison Eaton

Addison has twenty-six years of stories burning through her veins and a long list of lovers that pray they never come to life in text. She believes life's problems can be easily solved with a dark shade of lipstick, a cupcake, or a well timed joke. When she isn't stringing syllables together or chronicling her mishaps in love, she has dreams of becoming a librarian, writer, and dark over-lord. She spends her days working as a library media assistant, adventuring with her overweight corgi named Gatsby, and obtaining her second masters in Creative Writing.

Richa Gupta

Richa Gupta is a fifteen-year old girl living in Bangalore, India, with her parents and sister. She started devel-oping an interest in poetry from a young age, and has been honing her interest by writing and composing. She plans to publish a book of a collection of her poetry and short stories. Besides writing, she is also interested in western classical piano, Hindustani vocal and mathematics.

Erren Geraud Kelly

Erren Geraud Kelly is a poet based in Portland, Oregon. He has been writing for 25 years and has over 100 publi-cations in print and online such as *Hiram Poetry Review, Mudfish, Poetry Magazine* (online), *Ceremony, Cactus Heart, Similar Peaks, Gloom Cupboard, Poetry Salzburg* and others. His most recent publication is in Tipton Poetry Journal. He is also published in anthologies such as Fertile Ground, Beyond The Frontier and others. His work can also been seen on Youtube under the "Gallery Cabaret" links. He authored the chapbook "Disturbing The Peace" on *Night Ballet Press.* He received his B.A. in English-Creative Writing from Louisiana State University in Baton Rouge. He loves to read and travel, having visited 45 states, Canada and Europe.

Lauren Marshall

Lauren Marshall is a Canadian writer who is studying Creative Writing and Political Science at The University of British Columbia, Okanagan. She is the Creative Writing Assistant for the faculty, which entails aiding with visiting authors and hosting open mic nights for students and community members. Her works have been published in *The Dalhousie Review* and UBC Okanagan's *Paper Shell* anthology.

Carol Oberg

Carol Oberg began her writing career publishing with Blue Mountain Arts Inc. greeting cards for many years. She was one of three featured poets (10 works) in *Ancient Paths,* issue 16, and has published with *The Avocet, Burningword, Extract(s), Garbanzo, Harbinger Asylum,* and *The Fourth River,* among other literary journals. She and her husband are retired on a small inland lake in Michigan's Upper Peninsula.

Simon Perchik

Simon Perchik is an attorney whose poems have appeared in *Partisan Review, The Nation, Poetry, The New Yorker,* and elsewhere. His most recent collection is *Almost Rain,* published by River Otter Press (2013). For more information, free e-books and his essay titled "Magic, Illusion and Other Realities" please visit his website at www.simonperchik.com.

Priya Prithviraj

Priya Prithviraj is a major in English Literature at The English and Foreign Languages University in Hyderabad. She is involved in social work and she currently works with the Curriculum Development team at VOICE4Girls. She also volunteers for Teach for Change. She writes prose poems and on her blog at www.priyaprithviraj.blogspot.in.

Ty Stumpf

Ty Stumpf lives in Sanford, NC and is the Chair of the Humanities Department at Central Carolina Community College. Ty received his BA in English from Catawba College and his MA in English and creative writing from North Carolina State University. Ty and his wife, Bianka, have a son named Jude and a daughter named Cora.

Laryssa Wirstiuk

Laryssa Wirstiuk lives in Jersey City, NJ with her miniature dachshund Charlotte Moo. She teaches creative writing and writing for digital media at Rutgers University. Her work has been published or is forthcoming in *Crab Fat, Gargoyle Magazine, East Coast Literary Review,* and *Up the Staircase Quarterly.* You can view all her work at: www.laryssawirstiuk.com.

Visual Art

Annie Doan

Annie Doan is a visual artist based in Oklahoma City. Her work explores a sense of space and emotion through abstraction. The intertwining of her use of colors and lines creates a tension in the composition as if they're holding each other together within the space. The materials she uses often include watercolors, pen, and ink on birch boards. She has a background in Art Education and loves to stay involved in the art community. She is a very passionate advocate for children and the arts and has been a youth Instructor at Oklahoma Contemporary since 2013. Annie is currently at the University of Central Oklahoma where she is pursuing her B.A. in Art Education. Her ultimate goal is to encourage young artists to find themselves by incorporating art in their everyday lives. Annie has shown her artwork through collaborative and juried exhibitions throughout Oklahoma

Allen Forrest

Allen Forrest was born in Canada and bred in the U.S. He has created cover art and illustrations for many literary publications, he is the winner of the Leslie Jacoby Honor for Art at San Jose State University's *Reed Magazine* and his *Bel Red* painting series is part of the Bellevue College Foundation's permanent art collection. Forrest's expressive drawing and painting style is a mix of avant-garde expressionism and post-Impressionist elements reminiscent of van Gogh, creating emotion on canvas.

Sarah Katharina Kayß

Sarah Katharina Kayß, born in 1985 in Germany, studied Modern History in Germany and Britain. Her artwork, essays and poetry have appeared in literary magazines, journals and anthologies in Germany, Switzerland, Austria, the United Kingdom, Italy, Canada, New Zealand and the United States. Sarah is a recipient of the Austrian-VKSÖ Prize (2012) and winner of the manuscript-award of the German Writers Association for her poetry and essay collection *Ich mag die Welt so, wie sie ist* which was published in Munich, Germany in 2014. She edits the bilingual literature magazine *The Transnational* (www.the-transnational.com) and works on her doctorate at King's College London. www.SarahKatharinaKayss.com

Nicholas Perry

Nicholas Perry is an artist based out of Milwaukee, Wisconsin. A devoted abstractionist, his work is physical documentation of his experiences of memory. These experiences of memory are the sensations he felt during the event. His paintings and drawings present an unknown space to the viewers, removing reference to the real world and providing vulnerability for a true contemplative act.

Fiction

Liz Drayer

Liz Drayer is an attorney in Clearwater, Florida. Her short stories, essays and poems have appeared in the *Tampa Bay Times, Orlando Sentinel, Prick of the Spindle, Foliate Oak, Construction, Spitball,* and other publications. She lives with her husband and two daughters.

Toby Tucker Hecht

Toby Tucker Hecht is a scientist and short story writer who lives and works in Bethesda, Maryland. She is a previous contributor to *New Plains Review* and her fiction has also appeared in *The MacGuffin, The Baltimore Review, Epiphany, Bluestem* and other print and online literary journals.

Tammye Huf

Tammye Huf's work has appeared in *Necessary Fiction, Ginosko Literary Journal, Forge, The Storyteller,* and *Diverse Voices Quarterly.* She has worked as a teacher, a home educator, and an educational consultant. Having lived in the USA and Germany, she currently resides in England with her husband and three children where she is seeking publication for her first novel, *Butterfly Man.*

Brian Kamsoke

Brian Kamsoke is honored to be included in the *New Plains Review.* His most recent work has appeared in FICTION, *Reed Magazine,* REAL: *Regarding Arts & Letters, (Almost) Five Quarterly,* RKVRY *Quarterly Literary Journal, Flint Hills Review,* and *Pearl.* He was the recipient of the 2012-2013 MFA Creative Writing Fellowship at Wichita State University. He's currently working on a collection of short fiction as well as his first novel and a travel memoir. Visit www.briankamsoke.com.

Wandajune Bishop-Towle

Wandajune Bishop-Towle is a poet and licensed psychologist in Andover, MA. Her work has appeared in *PMS poemmemoirstory, Quiddy,* and *The Comstock Review,* among other journals. She is the proud mother of a young adult with autism, who is the frequent subject of her poetry.

Non-fiction

Matt Berman

Matt Berman writes stories about travel, work, and the world, bringing far-away readers into engaging natural world settings and real-life drama. Since 2003, he has worked seasonally on trail crews in America's National Parks, from the Grand Canyon to the Grand Tetons. His experience working outdoors in those wilderness cathedrals drives him to write about the physical interactions people have with places of natural beauty and how those events create meaning and connect us to the world we live in. Matt has an MFA in Writing Creative Non-Fiction from Spalding University in Louisville, Kentucky.

Dawn S. Davies

Dawn S. Davies is in her final year of the MFA program at Florida International University. She is the fiction editor of *Gulf Stream Magazine* at FIU and the graduate coordinator for the Writers on the Bay Reading Series. She has won some awards and residencies, including the Kentucky Women Writers Gabehart Prize for nonfiction and residencies with the Vermont Studio Center and Can Serrat. Her work has appeared in *Real South Magazine, River Styx, Brain, Child, Hippocampus, Cease, Cows,* and elsewhere, with pieces forthcoming in *Saw Palm, Ninth Letter,* and two in separate issues of *Fourth Genre.*

Richard LeBlond

Richard LeBlond is a biologist living in North Carolina, where he worked for that state's Natural Heritage Program until his retirement in 2007. He continues his biological research, and has begun writing about life experiences, travel to Europe and North Africa in the early 1970s, and more recent adventures in eastern Canada and the U.S. West. His essays have appeared in or been accepted by *Montreal Review, South85 blog, Cirque, Kudzu House, Carbon Culture Review* and *Weber — The Contemporary West.*

Morgan Sorrell

When Morgan Sorrell was a child, she wanted to be an artist, a singer, and an inventor. Since then, she's learned that an artist who invents new worlds through words is typically called a writer. She's currently attending the University of Central Oklahoma for a bachelor's degree in Creative Writing, and she's written three novels, along with numerous short stories. One of which, *The Write of Shame,* was recently published in the September 2014 issue of *Bacopa Review.*

Corinne Sullivan

Corinne Sullivan lives in Bronxville, where she is presently working as an Editorial Assistant for LUMINA. She holds a degree in English from Boston College, and she is an MFA candidate at Sarah Lawrence College. She has been previously published in *The Allegheny Review, Pithead Chapel, Rougarou,* and *Saturday Night*

Reader, and she has work forthcoming in *Night Train* and *Knee-Jerk.*